Fritz Kuhn, Bundesfuehrer *of the German American Bund*

AMERICA'S NAZIS

NAZIS

A Democratic Dilemma

AMERICA'S NAZIS

A Democratic Dilemma

A History of the German American Bund

by Susan Canedy

MARKGRAF PUBLICATIONS CROUP
PO Box 936 • Menlo Park, CA

E
184
G3
C363
1990

Markgraf Publications Group
a division of The Robots, Inc.
P.O. Box 936
Menlo Park, CA 94025

Printed and bound in the United States of America using premium quality,
neutral pH papers

ISBN 0-944109-06-3 Softcover
     0-944109-07-1 Hardcover
Library of Congress Card No. 88-063604

101743

Acknowledgments

This work was written over a period of several years and consequently has touched, and been touched by, many people. I would like to say thank you.

Thanks first to Sam Pignatella who gave me the idea to investigate the Bund. Thanks especially to Martin Kerr for acting as go-between to the National Socialist White People's Party; thanks to the former Bundists who agreed to talk to me and to share with me their experiences; without their assistance this book would not have come into existence.

During the research and writing period I received invaluable contributions. My thanks go to Bruce Ashkenas, on the staff of the National Archives, for assisting me in my efforts to turn a chaotic mass of documents and memorabilia into the heart of this work. Thanks also to the Honorable William Dickinson, to Major Stewart Wyland, Lieutenant Colonel Alfred Davis, Mr. Danny Carmichael, Mr. Scott Clark, and Ms Nancy Burford, for their help and assistance along the way.

Reviewing was accomplished, for the most part, by my doctoral committee. Thanks to Drs. Arnold Krammer, Larry Hill, Henry Dethloff, Dale Baum, and Kent Oots, all of Texas A&M University, for their time and expertise. This work stands as a tribute to their dedication to scholarship.

Finally, thanks to my family for their encouragement and support. Brigadier General (Ret.) and Mrs. Charles E. Canedy, Captain and Charles D. Canedy, Captain and Mrs. Russell Guillory, and especially Carolsue and Jacquelyn—I salute you.

FOREWORD

On a wintry day in February, 1939, more than 20,000 people, mostly German immigrants, crowded into New York's Madison Square Garden to listen to their *Fuehrer* speak. There he stood, Fritz Kuhn, on a stage festooned with American flags, dwarfed by an enormous picture of George Washington. Rows of uniformed troopers with swastika armbands lined the aisles and flanked the stage. It was a spectacle which remains etched in the memories of those who attended: an evening of patriotism and Germanness; isolationism and America First; rabid racism and anti-Semitism; and waves of thunderous applause following each tirade from the podium. The tumultuous event represented the high point of the four year history of the German-American Bund. Between 1936 and 1939 thousands of German-Americans, battered by the prejudice of World War One and the hopelessness of the Great Depression, found a satisfactory solution by joining the Bund. To many, it was a refuge—a home. Entire families could become involved: picnics and summer camps, German-language newspapers, and beerfests galore. Germans could gather to remember the Fatherland and bask in the distant radiance from the Third Reich.

If their giant rally in Madison Square Garden was the Bund's shining moment, it was also the beginning of their collapse. The meeting galvanized America against them. Hitler and the Nazi regime had thumbed their noses at the western democracies for years, walking out of the League of Nations, remilitarizing, expanding into Spain, Austria, and most recently, Czechoslovakia. Indeed, the German attack on Poland and the start of World War Two was but months away. America was growing fearful of the expanding menace in central Europe, and was increasingly convinced that Nazism would eventually have to be confronted. Saturday afternoon newsreels were filled with scenes of Nazi bullies and anti-Jewish riots which offended a large portion of America. It was one thing to watch columns of marching Nazis in the newsreels; it was quite another to see them gathering strength in America. In fact, the response to the Bund rally in Madison Square Garden was immediate. At the end of the evening, the exiting Bundists found themselves facing an angry crowd of nearly 100,000 people—only a wall of New York policemen protected them from their fellow Americans. It was clear that the German-American Bund was soon to dissolve. Whether it was due to Hitler's declaration of war on the U.S., the round-up of many Bundists as Alien Enemies, or the arrest of Fritz Kuhn on charges of embezzlement, is immaterial. Their prejudices and methods were rejected by the American public, and the Bund faded, unlamented, into historical obscurity.

Dr. Susan Canedy has resurrected this fascinating epoch for history buffs and professional scholars alike. She examines the pressures which created the Bund, and the appeal of Germany's siren call to its distant sons and daughters. Drawing upon actual documents, long buried in musty archives, and personal interviews with surviving Bund members, Dr. Canedy transports us back to the years of the Great Depression, as both the United States and Germany lurched to safety in their own ways. In America, Franklin Roosevelt's New Deal navigated through the difficult shoals of the 1930s with faith in democracy and concern for individual liberty; Hitler's Third Reich weathered the same period in cultural darkness and directionless persecution of it opponents, real and imagined.

American citizens living in Germany during the Nazi period quickly learned to remain silent, conform, or leave. Germans living in America, however, had the opportunity to voice their opinions and join together with others who shared their views. For many thousands of disgruntled Germans, a large percentage of whom were recent immigrants to the U.S., the answer was the German-American Bund. Unfortunately, its dual loyalties to both Washington and Berlin placed the Bund on a collision course with the events of the era. The volume which follows is an accurate and elegantly written examination of the Bund and its members. It is also a social history of America in the 1930s, as experienced by a disenchanted minority who felt they were strangers in a strange land.

Dr. Arnold Krammer
Professor of History
Texas A&M University

PREFACE

This is a story of many things: the isolation of a minority in pre-World War II America, the creation by that minority of a foreign and unpopular organization, and the ultimate demise of that minority by popular and governmental action. This is a chronicle of the German American Bund—an American Nazi group that operated in the United States from 1936-1941. It is an analysis of the movement's rise and fall, and, as such, serves to illustrate an era of American society and government as well.

The story of the German American Bund begins with German Americans. Although this is not a study of immigrant assimilation, the degree of assimilation that German Americans achieved in the 1920s played a major role in the formation of the Bund. German Americans, long a large and significant immigrant population, were firmly entrenched in American society by the coming of World War I. They embraced their Americanism and participated fully in all aspects of life in the United States while they nurtured their heritage in the form of cultural and social clubs and fraternities. However, this pattern changed abruptly with World War I. They were subjected to such harsh treatment during the war as suspected enemy aliens, that a segment of them would refuse integration into the general society. Clinging to their Germanness, this small portion of newly emigrated Germans embraced instead the national socialism developing in their homeland. The German American Bund arose directly from this group.

The German American Bund did not operate in a vacuum. Emerging in 1936, it was but one of many Fascist groups that played on the Depression and anti-Roosevelt sentiment. In historical retrospect, however, it must be seen quite apart from the likes of William Pelley's Silver Shirts or even Lawrence Dennis' American Fascism. The Bund was well in place by 1936, having taken over form and format from the Friends of New Germany which had roots back to 1924. Rather than basing its appeal on the turbulence created by the Great Depression, the Bund drew its membership and energy from a variety of precedential factors: a strong heritage of German American societies and a German American proclivity to socialize, the German American experience in World War I, World War I's effects on Germany, the Great Depression's effects on Germany, and the rise of Adolf Hitler. The German American Bund was a true sister movement of the NSDAP—more a product of Germany and German Americans than of America or American society.

Thus the German American Bund was able to capitalize on the insecurities and uncertainties which were prevalent in the German immigrant community and were exacerbated by the Great Depression. Under the leadership of Fritz Julius Kuhn, named by the press the American *Fuehrer*, the Bund developed a powerful and threatening image that impacted two continents. The image of Nazism presented by the Bund brought the reality of German Nazism to American shores, and while not a contributing factor to the United States' entrance into the war, the Bund certainly helped determine the American perception of the Third Reich.

America's perceptions of and attitudes toward Germany and German Americans were critical to the formation and life of the Bund. The experiences of the German American community during World War I contributed to the formation of this vocal and often vicious group of American Nazis as surely as America's fear of Fascism provided the mechanisms for its downfall. Due to the basic freedoms guaranteed to all American citizens, German Americans were free to gather together under the banner of American Fascism. The German American Bund's fate stands as a classic example of what happens to a group when it abuses those liberties.

CONTENTS

INTRODUCTION

The 1930s was a turbulent decade in history. World War I had indeed left its mark. The conclusion of this massive conflagration had brought about an uneasy realignment in the global balance of power. All major powers were faced with significant changes in their social, economic, and political structures, and the emergence of radical movements in Europe as well as in the United States was but one symbol of the economic instability and social factionalism that these transformations produced. A myriad of groups arose, spanning the political spectrum, to answer the prevalent confusion and dissatisfaction. In America, the German American Bund reacted to World War I and the accompanying social, political, and economic stresses with a program transplanted from Nazi Germany. An extremely visible and vocal group outfitted in the swastika and jackboots of the Third Reich, the Bund proposed National Socialism as a solution to the nation's ills. It was born, not of the Depression, but of social and political conditions prevalent in both Germany and the United States and can be traced back to the years of World War I.

World War I profoundly affected the German American community. While their harsh treatment during the war drove most to rapid assimilation, a segment would desperately cling to their ethnicity and attempt

1

to remain as culturally pure as possible for as long as possible. This group would endure the interwar years and all its conflicts as a separate entity. It is not surprising, then, to find this strand of German Americans dressed in the uniforms of the Third Reich some eighteen years later. German American Bundists stand not as Germans nor as Americans, but as a people caught in the limbo of assimilation. They represent the old order of Germany twisted by the major social conflicts prevalent in their homeland. They are as much a result of the historical treatment of German Americans in America as they are a product of the extreme social change of the 1920s and the 1930s.

Although it is impossible to single out any one event that led directly to the formation of the German American Bund, certainly World War I stands out as significant. This war impacted on individuals as well as on nations, and, as part of the historical continuum, tempered the times which followed it. Like most cataclysmic events, World War I started almost unobtrusively. A bullet aimed at the heir to the Austrian throne in the Balkan town of Sarajevo in July 1914 snuffed the life from Archduke Francis Ferdinand and ignited the world. It ushered in the world's first total war—a conflict that would involve vast armies and entire populations. State rose up against state, and nationality challenged nationality. Public perceptions were directed as much by propaganda as by the use of poison gas and diplomatic perfidy.

The United States, completing nearly 150 years of continental consolidation and economic expansion, watched with horror and surprise as the whole of Europe rapidly mobilized and plunged into war. Since the days of George Washington, neutrality had become an American ideal, and so it was declared. This was

Europe's war, not America's. President Woodrow Wilson urged the American public to be neutral in thought as well as in name, but it proved far easier preached than practised. True neutrality was never achieved, though this was due more to the beginnings of global interdependence than intent. Wartime exigencies and the realities of commerce dictated a neutrality that was often perceived as prejudicial. Relations between neutral and belligerent nations were characterized not by steady accommodation but by fluctuating tolerance.[1] Sentiment proved more predictable, however. From the outbreak of the war, the bulk of popular sympathy was for the Allies. Austria and Germany were seen as the aggressors as they had issued the first declarations of war. Even more influential in America's pro-Allied bias was its long tradition of cultural solidarity with the British and the awesome perception of Prussian militarism combined with the atrocity stories emanating out of Belgium.

In this situation, German Americans were faced with a peculiar crisis. America's declaration of neutrality resulted in a very tense atmosphere for the large segment of American society of German extraction. The United States Census of 1910 indicated that out of a total population of ninety-two million, there were 8,282,618 German Americans either born in Germany or of German-born parents. Although by no means an organized bloc, their large number and geographic concentration gave them the potential, both real and imagined, to exercise considerable political and social influence.

On the whole there is no question as to the loyalty of the vast bulk of German Americans. Whatever reasons had brought them to emigrate to the United States, all had come voluntarily. Some had come for land, others for business and agricultural opportunities, and still others for America's wide range of individual freedoms; America was the ideal of nations. In the years before World War I, German Americans were undoubtedly among the most solidly entrenched of all immigrant groups. They comprised an integral part of the machinery that ran finance capitalism, heavy industry, education, and agricultural and scientific research. Statistics show that Germans were among the most highly regarded nationalities because of their skill and diligence. Germans were rated first in self-control, moral integrity, and perseverance; second in physical vigor, intellectual ability, cooperation, and efficiency.[2] Such prominent German Americans as Chrysler, Studebaker, Rockefeller, Westinghouse, Heinz, and Weyerhauser, to name a few, were living proof of the stability and contributions of the German Americans. Moreover, they were anxious to assimilate, and by 1910 more than ninety percent of the German-born immigrants in the United States had taken out naturalization papers.

Following the outbreak of war in Europe in 1914, as the United States moved closer to active participation against the Central Powers, German Americans were faced with a wrenching conflict. Although solidly American, most were nonetheless German-born or -raised and felt a natural allegiance to the Fatherland. Despite the fact that this loyalty was usually nostalgic at best, they were increasingly linked with the Kaiser's perceived goal of world domination. More in defense of their safety in the American social system than in defense of the Kaiser or his global aspirations, a segment of the German American community went on the offensive. Their efforts had disastrous results.

The German language press in America accepted Germany's explanation for the outbreak of war and denounced the pro-Allied bias of most American news coverage. German press organs demanded strict neutrality and waged an editorial war against anti-German propaganda. As the United States had declared a neutral stance, the German American community acted out of a sense of patriotism—demonstrating, they thought, their belief in democracy.

The best known American defender of Germany during this time was George Sylvester Viereck. Born in Germany but raised in America, Viereck published a widely circulated English-language weekly newspaper, *The Fatherland*.[3] Emanating from Viereck's deep-seated belief in German power and equality, it urged German Americans to take united action against what it perceived to be the obvious bias of the American position.[4] *The Fatherland* claimed it was presenting Germany's arguments not because German Americans owed allegiance to the Kaiser, but because of the belief that German Americans, as Americans, should exercise their rights of political and cultural freedom as espoused by the Constitution.[5] Regardless of its intent, the newspaper's extreme pro-German stance only helped to polarize American opinion against German Americans. Even though the majority of German Americans were unattracted by such appeals, this upsurge of chauvinism by a tiny but vocal sector produced new community interest in cultural societies while it attracted the growing suspicion of the general population.

The German American movement during the First World War was not an organized movement as such, but a diverse group of cultural organizations. Outside the amorphous National German-American Alliance, covered below, most German Americans were grouped together out of convenience and culture. In fact, German Americans congregated readily. They had, as a group, maintained a plethora of segregated social clubs since the beginning of the immigrant waves before the American Revolution.[6] These associations eased the cultural shock that awaited newly transplanted peoples and facilitated assimilation. During World War I there were of course, fringe organizations such as the German University League, comprised of former students of German universities, the Pan-German Alliance, and the Educational Alliance for the Preservation of German Culture in Foreign Lands. These were not tightly organized nor politically potent, but were merely interest groups bound by cultural rather than political purpose. All were understandably inactive during the hysterical patriotism of the war.

The spearhead of German Americans, if they can be grouped together, was the National German-American Alliance. Organized in 1901 by Charles John Hexamer, a civil engineer in Philadelphia, the Alliance represented a federation of existing German American organizations and boasted a membership of approximately two million.[7] A total of forty states claimed at least one chapter with the greatest numerical strength lying in Pennsylvania, Wisconsin, New York, Ohio, Indiana, Illinois, and Iowa. According to its constitution, the Alliance existed to promote the common good of German Americans, bring together citizens of German descent, and protect against nativist attack. Its aim was primarily cultural; a thirteen point program prohibited political involvement by its officers and forbade religious activities.[8] Due to its cultural attraction and the nationalistic feeling prevalent at the turn of the century, the Alliance became the largest ethnic organization in the United States.

Largely financed by the brewing interests to combat the public movement toward Prohibition, the Alliance was able to harness its membership and marshal what appeared to be massive political strength. Declaring that the Prohibition movement was directed at German "manners and customs, the joviality of the German people . . . ," the Alliance went on the defensive as Prohibition gained national strength.[9] Indeed, Prohibition was the sole *raison d'etre* of local Alliances before the war; the Anti-Saloon League did more to build the Alliance than did lovers of German culture in the United States. Owing to the financial strength of its major contributors, the Alliance widened its scope of activities and openly crusaded for the maintenance of American neutrality in the World War.

Whatever its original focus, the Alliance was clearly a large group with considerable political muscle. It was strong enough to lobby, albeit ineffectively, against munitions exports, various arms embargoes, and American loans to England. But after Wilson's re-election in 1916, the Alliance found itself fighting an increasingly strong and hostile public undercurrent. Fervently anti-Wilson, much of its clout had dissolved with his re-election and the "hyphen loyalty" question, which became a patriotic issue during that election. The Alliance hoped to gain some lost ground by turning to its propaganda press. In its war against what it perceived as an Anglo-American entente, the Alliance cooperated extensively with propagandists from Germany. Far from mobilizing additional support, however, such actions only convinced the American public of German American ties to the Fatherland and fueled the belief of widespread subversion and espionage.

Germany's proclamation of unrestricted submarine warfare, followed by the revelation of the Zimmermann telegram in February 1917, solidified American opinion and brought all things German under suspicion. The declaration of war in April spelled the end of the National German-American Alliance. For nearly three years it had championed Germany's cause, but found it impossible to protect itself from growing anti-German sentiment.[12]

Although most German Americans quickly discarded their *Deutschtum* with the American declaration of war, it was of little avail in the face of the unbridled emotionalism unleashed against them. Allied propaganda machinery was unremitting and merciless in its portrayal of German soldiers as monstrous beasts, criminal barbarians, and treacherous Huns.[11] Tales of espionage and sabotage, some true, reinforced the image of German Americans as the willing pawns of the Kaiser. The German Americans in the United States found themselves living in a hostile environment, and there was little they could do.

It was not only public sentiment which German Americans had to fear, but their government as well. With the tacit endorsement of the Wilson cabinet, Attorney General Thomas Gregory bestowed semi-official status on the American Protective League (APL) in 1917. The APL, a private organization established by Chicago advertising executive Albert Briggs, was composed of some 200,000 untrained, volunteer detectives whose mission was to feed the Justice Department with information about suspected aliens. Although possessing no formal statutory authority to make arrests, members paid one dollar to receive a badge and waged a vigorous crusade against disloyalty.[12] The APL conducted thousands of investigations, none of which exposed a single bona fide spy. It did succeed, however, in fueling the climate of suspicion and alarm.

The American Protective League was not the only agency German Americans had to fear. For example, of note was the Committee on Public Information.

Created by executive order in April 1917, and chaired by the untiring George Creel, this committee was to coordinate the government's propaganda effort to sell the war. By tying together the war aims of the home front and the battle front, Creel effectively harnessed public opinion through a massive advertising campaign which included photos, movies, exhibits, and posters.[13] Creel made every effort to work with and through German American groups rather than at their expense; any attention afforded Germany was passed on to German Americans in the form of intolerance.

The activities of the APL and the Committee on Public Information were only symptoms of the Germanophobia that swept the United States with America's entry into the war. Anti-German sentiment spanned the spectrum of everyday life. German Shepherd dogs were renamed Alsatians, the Frankfurter became the hot dog, Sauerkraut turned into liberty cabbage and the like. Hysterical stories circulated about Germans posing as Bible salesmen who tried to stir up blacks in the South; and the militia in Dayton, Ohio, guarded the city waterworks against acts of German sabotage. German-speaking Red Cross workers were rumored to have put bacteria in medical supplies; and Cincinnati's meat packers were suspected of grinding glass into their sausages. Street and town names were changed overnight, and the German language was forbidden in schools, churches, and in public places.

Dissent in the United States had become not only disloyal and dangerous but illegal as well. Never had patriotism reached so feverish a pitch. The night before his request for a declaration of war on April 6, 1917, President Wilson warned that if the country was led into war, it would "forget there ever was such a thing as tolerance."[14] For millions of terrified German Americans, his words were soon to prove sadly true.

The months following the United States' entry into the war were a period of tribulation for millions of German-born immigrants. There was no sympathy for the division of loyalties which most German Americans had to reconcile. The war had split their German-ism from their Americanism and was for most as catastrophic as the military conflict being waged in Europe. As hyphenated citizens, German Americans would bear the brunt of America's perception of the Huns' invasion of civilized Europe.

Congress reflected and encouraged the hysteria by passing draconian laws for the suppression of dissent. Measures such as the Espionage Act of June 1917, the Sabotage Act of April 1918, and the Sedition Act of May 1918 were harsh beyond any previous legislation. This federal legislation imposed fines and imprison-ment for those suspected of espionage, sabotage, or otherwise obstructing the war effort. Postal officials were granted the authority to determine what printed matter was seditious or treasonable, thus regulating the mails; and words or deeds perceived as intended to induce contempt for the United States were punishable both by fine and imprisonment. Vigorously and often capriciously enforced, these measures, aimed at disci-plining the disloyal, were almost as stern as any lynch mob could desire.

In the fall of 1917, Wilson ordered all German aliens over the age of fourteen to register with the govern-ment, and all property owned by German aliens became subject to government control. While these measures were tolerable to most Americans caught up in the war hysteria, such mandates were easily abused. The most serious cases of such abuse were conducted immediately after the war by Attorney General A. Mitchell Palmer. As overall custodian of federal judi-cial policy, and formerly Alien Property Custodian,

Palmer became notorious for his aggressive tactics to eliminate German-owned businesses in the United States. Riding on a tide of xenophobia, Attorney General Palmer used his awesome power to conduct raids on radical aliens, rounding up thousands and holding them without legal safeguards. This abuse of power and the injustice visited upon the minority was as alarming as the general suppression of free thought and action that accompanied such practices.[15]

This federal activity only mirrored steps taken on the state and local levels. Once the spirit of intolerance was unleashed, containing it was an impossible task. Pro-German "offenders" who escaped the federal acts were likely to be caught in the labyrinth of state sedition laws or to suffer the wrath of vigilantes and self-proclaimed patriots. Local patriots took direct action by harassing unpopular groups and controversial figures. A great many private groups emerged, from the superpatriotic American Defense Society to the spy-chasing Knights of Liberty, Sedition Slammers, and the Boy Spies of America.[16] The most dangerous were the state and local Councils of National Defense. Spawned by the national Council of National Defense which was created by Congress in August 1916, these lower councils, some of which were granted the authority to subpoena witnesses and punish for contempt, numbered 184,000 nationwide and were fervid in the performance of their duties against disloyal activities. Using secret informers and guilt by association, these councils became notorious for their vigilante methods.[17]

Anti-German hysteria swept the nation. The most notorious disseminator was John Ratham, editor of the Rhode Island *Providence Journal*, who thundered that German and Austrian aliens should be considered spies unless proved otherwise.[18] Going a step further,

Reverend Newell Dwight Hillis of the Plymouth Congregational Church of Brooklyn, New York, pronounced from the pulpit his belief that Germans were genetically defective and proposed a plan to exterminate the German people by sterilizing ten million German men.[19] Often making reference to German American stupidity and treason, he spiced his well-attended sermons with lurid tales and pornographic references.

Harassment of German Americans became commonplace. Suspicion escalated to threats of violence, acts of vandalism, tar and feather ceremonies, forced marches, and flag kissing. Surprisingly, there is only one substantiated death—the lynching murder of Robert Paul Prager in Collinsville, Illinois, on 5 April 1918.[20] Anti-German hysteria ran at such a fevered pitch that it is incredible that not many more German Americans were killed.

In the face of this hysteria, German Americans donated generously to the American war chest, exceeded their Liberty Loan quotas, spearheaded loan drives, generally cooperated with conscription, and demonstrated themselves bravely on the battlefield. Such measures were generally ignored by the public, however. Anti-German sentiment continued unchecked, and the hostility which surrounded them scarred German America and contributed substantially to the later emergence of Fritz Kuhn and the German American Bund.

The intolerance levied against German Americans during the First World War was not repeated with such intensity during the Second. The memories remained, however. These drove the vast majority of German Americans to assimilate quickly and quietly. Only a small segment of German America would answer Germany's second call to arms, and their reactions and movements were tempered by the actions of the past.

The German American Bund was as much a product of the harsh treatment of German Americans during the World War as it was an arm of the Nazi movement. Moreover, it was the product of the economic and social dislocations of the years between the wars. Necessarily, then, an understanding of conditions in both Germany and the United States during the interwar years is crucial to the study of the Bund.

ENDNOTES
Introduction

1. American neutrality during the years 1914-1917 has been covered in great detail. An examination of the literature can lead only to one conclusion, that neutrality is a very difficult ship to steer. Realistically, true neutrality is rarely achieved due to actual contingencies of wartime commerce and relations. While it may have been Washington's intent to remain totally impartial and relatively aloof from Europe's warring policies, geography, established trade patterns, military circumstances, and personalities often circumvented this desire. An analysis of changing interpretations of American neutrality may be found in Richard W. Leopold, "The Problem of American Intervention, 1917: An Historiographical Retrospective," *World Politics* 2 (1950): 405-25; Daniel M. Smith, "National Interest and American Intervention, 1917: An Historiographical Appraisal," *Journal of American History* 52 (1965): 5-24. See also, Ross Gregory, *The Origins of American Intervention in the First World War* (New York: W. W. Norton and Company, Inc., 1971); Arnold A. Offner, *The Origins of the Second World War: American Foreign Policy and World Politics, 1917-1941* (New York: Praeger Publishers, 1975); Patrick Devlin, *Too Proud to Fight: Woodrow Wilson's Neutrality* (New York: Oxford University Press, 1975); Harvey A. DeWeerd, *President Wilson Fights His War: World War I and the American Intervention* (New York: The Macmillan Company, 1968).

2. Howard B. Woolston, "Rating the Nations: A Study in the Statistics of Opinion," *American Journal of Sociology* 22 (November 1916): 381-90.

3. Weekly circulation peaked at 100,000, leveling off in 1915 to 75,000, the largest circulation of any pro-German propaganda tract in America.

4. For a detailed description and examination of Viereck, with emphasis on the man and his activities, see Niel M. Johnson, *George Sylvester Viereck* (Chicago: University of Illinois Press, 1972).

5. *The Fatherland*, 31 August 1914, p. 12.

6. For a good overview of German American cultural unity see Gordon A. Craig, *The Germans* (New York: G. P. Putnam's Sons, 1982); and Adolph Schalk, *The Germans* (Englewood Cliffs, N. J.: Prentice-Hall, Inc., 1971). An authoritative work in the field of German ethnicity is Albert B. Faust, *The German Element in the United States* (Salem, N. H.: Ayer Company Publishers, Inc., 1927) which covers the period to 1925. See also Thomas Sowell, *Ethnic America* (New York: Basic Books, Inc., 1981); Theodore Huebener, *The Germans in America* (New York: Chilton Co., 1962); Carl Wittke, *We Who Built America: The Saga of the Immigrant* (Cleveland: Press of Case Western Reserve University, 1964); Maxine Seller, "To Seek America," *A History of Ethnic Life in the United States* (Englewood Cliffs, N. J.: Jerome S. Ozer, 1977). Broader studies incorporating ethnicity and nativism include John Higham, *Send These to Me: Jews and Other Immigrants in Urban America* (New York: Atheneum, 1975) and *Strangers in the Land: Patterns of American Nativism, 1860-1925* (New York: Atheneum, 1963); Robert D. Parmet, *Labor and Immigration in Industrial America* (Boston: Twayne Publishers, 1981); and Edward George Hartmann, *The Movement to Americanize the Immigrant* (New York: AMS Press, 1967).

7. Clifton J. Child, *The German-Americans in Politics* (New York: Arno Press and the *New York Times*, 1970), p. 4. This is a detailed history of the Alliance and its inception. For a less favorable look at the Alliance see Frederick C. Luebke, *Bonds of Loyalty: German-Americans and World War I* (DeKalb, Ill.: Northern Illinois University Press, 1974).

8. LaVern J. Rippley, *The German Americans* (Boston: Twayne Publishers, 1976), p. 180.

9. Quoted from Richard O'Connor, *The German Americans* (Boston: Little, Brown and Company, 1968), p. 386.

10. In January 1918, Senator William Henry King of Utah introduced a Congressional bill to repeal the charter of the National German-American Alliance. A sub-committee of the Senate Committee on the Judiciary was appointed to consider the actions of the Alliance during the war. These hearings were held between 23 February and 13 April. On 11 April the executive committee of the Alliance met and agreed to dissolve the national convention and turn its funds over to the American Red Cross.

11. British propaganda utilized such facts as the invasion of Belgium and the sinking of the *Lusitania* with telling effect. Most items did not have to be embellished to serve British purposes. A great advantage that the British had over German propaganda was the use of a common language and strict censorship of all cables to the United States. See M. L. Sanders and Philip M. Taylor, *British Propaganda during the First World War, 1914-18* (London: The Macmillan Press ltd., 1982); George G. Bruntz, *Allied Propaganda and the Collapse of the German Empire in 1918* (Stanford: Stanford University Press, 1938); H. C. Peterson, *Propaganda for War: The Campaign against American Neutrality, 1914-1917* (Norman, Ok.: University of Oklahoma Press, 1939); and Harold D. Lasswell, *Propaganda Technique in World War I* (Cambridge: The M.I.T. Press, 1971).

12. See Paul L. Murphy, *World War I and the Origin of Civil Liberties in the US* (New York: W. W. Norton and Company, 1979), pp. 89-90.

13. See George Creek, *How We Advertized America* (New York: Harper and Brothers, 1920). Also, James R. Mock and Cedric Larson, *Words that Won the War: The Story of the Committee on Public Information, 1917-1919* (Princeton: Princeton University Press, 1939); Stephen L. Vaughn, *Holding Fast the Inner Lines: Democracy, Nationalism and the Committee on Public Information* (Chapel Hill, N. C.: University of North Carolina Press, 1980).

14. The full quote is, "Once lead this people into war, and they'll forget there ever was such a thing as tolerance. To fight you must be brutal and ruthless, and the spirit of ruthless brutality will enter into the very fibre of our national life, infecting Congress, the courts, the policeman on the beat, the man in the street." As quoted in Arthur S. Link, *Woodrow Wilson and the Progressive Era 1910-1917* (New York: Harper and Row, 1954), p. 277. The original found in Ray Stannard Baker, *Woodrow Wilson: Life and Letters* (New York: 1927-39), VI, p. 490.

15. An excellent overview of the various discussions of the dimensions of World War I civil liberties violations is H. C. Peterson, *Opponents of War 1917-1918: The Story of the Persecution of Anti-War Groups* (Seattle: University of Washington Press, 1968). See also William Preston, Jr., *Aliens and Dissenters: Federal Suppression of Radicals, 1903-1933* (New York: Harper and Row, 1966); Harry N. Scheiber, *The Wilson Administration and Civil Liberties, 1917-1921* (Ithaca, N. Y.: Cornell University Press, 1960); and Zechariah Chafee, Jr., *Free Speech in the United States* (Cambridge, Mass.: Harvard University Press, 1941).

16. Paul Murphy, *WWI and the Origin of Civil Liberties in the US*, pp. 86-7.

17. Ibid., pp. 86-9.

18. Frederick Luebke, *Bonds of Loyalty*, p. 243.

19. Reverend Newell Dwight Hillis published his lectures in two volumes as *The Blot on the Kaiser's 'Scutcheon* (New York: Fleming H. Revell, 1918) and *German Atrocities: Their Nature and Philosophy* (New York: Fleming H. Revell, 1918).

20. The story of the Prager murder is found in Frederick G. Luebke's *Bonds of Loyalty*.

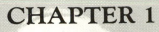

CHAPTER 1

THE
SEEDBED

CHAPTER 1

THE SEEDBED

In order to understand the motivations and significance of a group such as the German American Bund, which emerged during the Depression era, one must appreciate the social, economic, and political stresses present in American and German societies in the 1920s and 1930s. These were years that laid the foundations for the Bund. Although it emerged later, the Bund rested on the changes and accompanying anxieties and fears that coursed through the decade of the 1920s. Each of the conflicts that marked this period—war/peace, urban/rural, machine/man, immigrant/nativist, wet/dry, black/white—in some way encouraged the growth of this radical Nazi group. The onset of the Great Depression only exacerbated these transitional imbalances.

The German American Bund was an American group composed almost wholly of newly emigrated German citizens. These people, as immigrants, were ultrasensitive to the changes occurring in American society. Moreover, their sense of normalcy was markedly distinct from that of old stock Americans. Their perceptions of the "good old days" were drastically different from those held by the majority of the populace. Their assimilation into American society was determined not only by their adopted environment but also by conditions prevalent in their homeland. There was, perhaps, no way they could deal with this myriad of stress and move easily into the mainstream of society.

In the United States, the 1920s was a decade of extremes and imbalances. It was an age of prosperity and poverty, hope and frustration, calm and violence, leisure and lawlessness. These conditions were uneasily juxtaposed and heightened by the social and economic upheavals occurring during the era. This time has been characterized as the Jazz Age by some, emphasizing a seeming change in morality and women's roles, and freedoms bought by money and mobility to enjoy such marvels as the automobile and nightclub. To others the 1920s stand out as the Age of Dismay as they discover a gaudy facade masking increased crime, degeneracy, and a decadent old order.

It was certainly a volatile age. America was forced to address several crucial issues and make the transition into what is loosely called the twentieth, or modern, century. World War I was over. American society had to demobilize and make the transition to peace. Additionally, by 1920 a majority of the population lived in communities with more than 2500 residents. People had to adjust their lifestyles and adapt themselves to urban living. Technological advancements went hand in hand with a growing population. Moreover, Prohibition was enacted in 1919. This produced a further alteration in lifestyle and the glorification of a heretofore seamier side of society. All these progressions had to be reconciled. It was not an easy transition.

Into this maelstrom of social and economic change a portion of German immigrants would be thrust. They would come to make up the nucleus that later became the German American Bund. But, as will be seen, this was only a small segment of the German American community. Their compatriots, for the most part, had necessarily quickly assimilated with the conclusion of World War I. There would remain a portion, however, that, deeply affected by the intolerance they suffered during the war, would cling to their Germanness. They would, in turn, be affected not only by change in America but also by change in Germany. And change in both countries was due in large part to the waging of World War I and its aftermath.

Indeed, in the United States and Germany, much of the tone of the 1920s was set by the effects of the World War.[1] It had been modern civilization's first total war and it profoundly influenced the people and institutions which survived it. The destruction left in the wake of the war was enormous. Europe had nearly bled to death. Millions of tons of shipping had been sunk, forests burnt, great tracts of arable land laid waste, cities gutted, and industrial production virtually halted. Approximately eight million men lost their lives on the battlefields and millions more returned home maimed.[2] Countless people were left homeless. A generation was profoundly affected; rare was the family not touched by death or wounds. In the end, Europe had lost both the population and the means of production to sustain life as she had known it.

Of the combatants, the United States alone emerged relatively unscathed. Her participation in the conflict, comprising two hundred days of combat at a cost of 50,000 men, and more than 200,000 wounded, had fueled her economy and increased the efficiency of her industrial base.[3] Indeed, at the conclusion of the war that ended European global hegemony, the United States emerged as the premier power. Yet the general mood in the United States following World War I favored a return to "normalcy." War had changed Americans, and most were anxious to get back to life as

they had known it. Following the conflict, the United
States sought to disengage her economy and society
from all things related to war. As a result she traumati-
cally moved through two trying years of demobiliza-
tion and reconversion and launched a desperate search
for security at home and abroad.[4] The much-sought-
after normalcy proved an enigma, however. The 1920s
witnessed the collapse of the old order simultaneously
with the highly stressful introduction of modernity.
There was no turning back to what had been; as the
times had changed, so too had the reality of normalcy.

The 1920 presidential election brought the rejection
of Woodrow Wilson and his idealistic international-
ism, and the election of "Uncle" Warren G. Harding
and conservative parochialism. The United States
immediately came off her war-footing, hastily demobil-
ized, restructured her economy to favor consumer
industries, and rejected thoughts of international
guardianship. Highly disillusioned, Washington cast
off the role of protector of the peace and supported
neither the Treaty of Versailles nor the League of
Nations. Giving priority to domestic reconstruction,
she thus inadvertently weakened the victors and
opened the door to an alliance of vengeful power in the
defeated.[5]

Economically, the 1920s was a decade of growing
prosperity. Relatively brief post-war depressions hit in
1921 and later in 1924 and 1927, but generally by 1922
the economy appeared strong. Increased national production, especially in the area of consumer goods, and
relatively stable price levels invigorated the economy.
Business prospered; government controls were lifted
and both small and large establishments profited.
Freed from the restraints of wartime restrictions, consumer industries flourished as people moved to recapture the "good old days."

This prosperity was marred, however, and severely skewed, by the effects of industrialism and rapid urbanization. World War I had catalyzed and heightened the industrial movement, and with the rush to provide material demanded by war had come mass migrations into the cities and spectacular urban growth.[6] This movement into the cities and factories often resulted in crowded, poor, and unhealthy living and working conditions while it intensified working-class consciousness and spawned a move to unionization and radicalism. The advent of the Machine Age produced severe dislocations, and people struggled to maintain their individuality in the face of mechanization. Moreover, the technological advancements that created increased production and economic prosperity were accompanied by relatively high technological unemployment as machines replaced skilled human labor. It is estimated that the rate of unemployment for the period averaged between 10-13%.[7] Even in the prosperous year of 1929 a majority of workers' families lived dangerously close to the poverty level.[8] While the issue of unemployment excited little general interest, it contributed to the labor unrest endemic to the decade. Labor unrest erupted as early as 1919; it is estimated that that year alone witnessed over 3000 strikes.[9] While laborers suffered the indignations and hardships that accompanied rising production, extravagance and a bright, gaudy culture beckoned them from the other side of the tracks. Electrical appliances and automobiles were but two material innovations that spread rapidly through the middle and upper classes and portrayed a drastically unequal distribution of income and opportunity.

With the black migration north to the industrial sites, racial tensions increased as well and erupted in a series of riots in the summer of 1919 in such places as

Chicago, Charleston, and Knoxville.[12] Old, never-forgotten prejudices had been reinvigorated with the rebirth of the Ku Klux Klan in 1915 in Stone Mountain, Georgia. The Klan marched in the eerie silence of the night throughout the 1920s as high national stress likewise produced radical movements of all political shades.[11]

The Socialist Party, wracked by internal strife, struggled for a foothold as the American Communist Party, formed in September 1919, worked to gain legitimacy on foreign soil amid intense hostility.[12] The Red Scare that erupted around and because of Communist activities engendered a fear of all radical or "un-American" groups. Recent immigrants and unassimilated minority groups once again came under suspicion, and the public demanded and received restricted immigration legislation. This in turn fostered the rise of the super-patriots—people who embraced "100% Americanism" to quell their fears of the growing political extremism. Patriotism came to mean national isolation and prejudice against all things foreign. The precedent for this attitude had been set during the war years when America, consolidating herself to fight "Europe's war," had unleashed a campaign of hatred against all those with suspected ties to the enemy. After the war, this ethnic hatred only seemingly abated. The term 100% American was coined to designate "good" Americans or those with "absolute" loyalties. Groups such as the American Legion, organized in France in February 1919 and brought to the United States a few months later, devoted themselves to "real" American ideals and proved themselves diligent hyper-patriotic counterforces.[13]

This was indeed an uneasy period. Yoga, Ouiga boards, Freudianism, and an escape to a bohemian lifestyle all characterized a society caught between two Ages. The 1920s were a transition decade—a period of time of change in attitudes and perceptions as the United States moved unsteadily into the twentieth century. The development from a predominantly agriculturally based state to a principal industrial nation demanded changes in lifestyles, occupations, and habitat from her people. It was not a transition easily made.

Against this backdrop of social change, the stock market collapsed in October 1929. The Great Depression was on.[14] Prices dropped sharply, foreign trade fell off, factories cut production or shut down, real estate values declined, banks failed, wages were cut, and the unemployment rate accelerated rapidly. The GNP dropped from $104.4 billion in 1929 to $74.2 billion in 1933. Farm prices, low at the outset, fell sixty-one percent between those years. Exports declined sixty-eight percent for the same period, and imports diminished as well. General unemployment rose from 3.1 percent in 1929 to over 25 percent in 1933.

These statistical figures, by no means complete, do not give a picture of the Depression in human terms.[15] Basic needs were major problems among the people most affected. Many actually starved to death in what was the most prosperous nation on the earth. Rising percentages of underweight school children were reported, and diseases related to malnutrition increased significantly. The nation's housing standards severely deteriorated. Construction virtually stopped and people could not afford to buy or rent. Doubling up with friends or relatives was common, and a sharp increase in the number of homeless and wandering manifested itself. Statistics indicate a decline in new families in the 1930s; existing families reported a significantly lower birth rate and an increase in the incidence of family desertion. As the economy shattered, so did people's lives. As one historian has noted, the collapse of the economy not only meant bankrupt businesses, food shortages in the big cities, and unemployment, but, "it had the effect, which is the unique quality of economic catastrophe, of reaching down to and touching every single member of the community in a way which no political event can."[16]

Unwilling to break the American spirit of self-reliance, and operating under the commonly-held belief that depression was a natural consequence of prosperity and would run itself out, President Herbert Hoover moved slowly and cautiously into the crisis for which he was unfairly blamed.[17] Breaking the precedent of presidential inactivity regarding government activity during depression, Hoover suggested the coordination of business and government agencies and enlisted the active cooperation of state governments and Chambers of Commerce in programs designed to aid recovery. Despite the fact that Hoover was far more active than his predecessors, his programs hardly committed the federal government to a major role. Measures such as the Agricultural Marketing Act, the National Credit Corporation, the Reconstruction Finance Corporation, and the Emergency Relief and Reconstruction Act barely stemmed the tide of depression while it fueled the fire of the opposition.

By 1932, with hardship widespread and no obvious relief in sight, Herbert Hoover was turned out of office and replaced by the dynamic Franklin D. Roosevelt who promised to use governmental power to whatever extent necessary to reverse the disastrous economic trends. Although a detailed discussion of Roosevelt's New Deal policies is not technically relevant to this study, it is important to understand the emotional climate that it produced in its wake.[18] Roosevelt succeeded where Hoover failed in that he invigorated morale. By and large, Roosevelt performed as promised in that he did use wide governmental power in his attempt to stem the tide of the depression. He did not cure the nation's economic ills, however; it took the massive deficit spending of World War II to put the nation back on a sound economic footing.

Throughout his first term, Roosevelt created agencies and instituted recovery measures that intertwined public and private life as never before. Government agencies were created to provide relief, to stimulate economic activity, and to reform the system to avoid future depressions. Programs set up were directed toward saving American political and economic institutions. On the whole they were improvisations drawn up to meet specific needs.[19] As they were expanded to ensure lasting reform, the role of government in public life likewise expanded, transforming the United States into an economic and social welfare state.

Considering that the effects of the Depression were so far-reaching and that the majority of the population experienced deprivation for a relatively extended period of time, one of the wonders of the age is that there was no wide-spread revolutionary upsurge. Dissatisfaction was general, but for the most part passive. Most of the basic unrest found expression in a reaffirmation of Americanism. People clung to imaginary ideals of democracy in order to right perceived wrongs—economic, social, and political.

Although the majority of the American populace cheered Roosevelt's prescriptions, the increased governmental control and intervention heightened some people's fears of socialism, whereas others wrote

off capitalism as a failure and marched into the socialist camp. In the years prior to World War II, hundreds
of reactionary and radical groups, spanning the
extremes of the political spectrum, sprang up to counter the administration's proposed political agenda.[20]
And, as in the period prior to and during World War I, a
segment of American society polarized, and so-called
superpatriots emerged to combat these groups and
keep vigilant watch for suspected "un-Americans."

A portion of these "un-Americans" would be German
Americans—once again under the public gaze as the
second of the great wars approached. Although the
vast majority of the German American community,
recalling their vulnerability and experiences during
World War I, quickly and quietly slipped into the melt-
ing pot of American society, a small percentage, mostly
recent immigrants to the United States, promoted the
Fascism of their homeland.

In sharp contrast to the United States, Germany's
post-war evolution was extremely traumatic. World
War I had virtually decimated Germany. After four
years of total war, Germany was left with nearly five
million casualties, a prostrate economy, and a
government deeply in debt. To the populace, there was
no turning away from the effects of the war.[21] Industrial activity virtually ceased, deprived of the life-
giving raw materials and labor force which fueled it.
Unemployment rose and inflation soared. Personal
savings were quickly exhausted and food was scarce.
Order and stability were as illusive as the peace. A
warring mentality remained, born of hardship and
deprivation. Revolts spread throughout the country,
and at all levels of government hastily elected bodies
calling themselves soldiers', sailors', and workers'
councils assumed power in the resulting vacuum. What

order there was was maintained by the Freikorps, quasi-military units of volunteers organized by senior officers of the old Army.[22] Under their bayonets, leftist revolutionary cells were disbanded and the Weimar Republic was sheltered. In this atmosphere of reaction, chaos, and collapse, right-wing nationalism flourished and militarism revived.

Upon this maelstrom of devastation the Treaty of Versailles was imposed. It was six months from the signing of the armistice that ended the war to the presentation of the peace terms. German representatives were not allowed to participate in the negotiations and had clung to President Wilson's Fourteen Point program as a guarantee against their enemies' extreme demands. Wilson's proposals included such ideals as openly arrived covenants of peace, impartial adjustment of colonial claims, and the formation of a general assembly of nations—undeniably the epitome of a just peace.

Not surprisingly, Germany had been quite unprepared to lose the war. Perhaps no nation prepares for the possibility of military defeat. Instead of accepting defeat when acknowledged by the military command, Germany countered with the "stab in the back" theory—the theory that the war could have been won were it not for cells of internal treachery. Faced with French and British demands for a harsh peace settlement so as to prevent further German resurgence, Germany clung to Wilson's idealism. As an American observer wrote in May 1919, "The German people had been led to believe that Germany had been unluckily beaten after a fine and clean fight owing to the ruinous effect of the blockade on home morale, and perhaps too far-reaching plans of her leaders, but that happily President Wilson could be appealed to, and would arrange a compromise peace satisfactory to Germany."[23] With this attitude prevalent in Germany, the actual presentation of the peace terms had a devastating effect.

Germany was to lose twelve percent of her population and thirteen percent of her territory, including three-fourths of her iron ore and one-fifth of her coal. The Saar was to be French for fifteen years to end with a plebiscite, and the Rhineland would remain under Allied military occupation for a similar period. No colonies were to be restored. Germany was to pay reparations in cash and in kind of an unspecified value. She was to disarm and was denied entrance into the League of Nations. Adding insult to injury, Germany was branded with the guilt of having caused the war, and her war leaders were to be tried for war crimes.[24] With the stroke of a pen, Germany had lost her imperial glory.

In reality, the provisions of the Treaty of Versailles were not unduly harsh nor restrictive. Although it did not embody Wilson's call for a new world order, neither did it reflect the extreme French or British desires for retaliation. Given Germany's attitude, however, the cumulative effect of the territorial changes and punitive clauses was tremendous. Presented as a *Diktat* to the new Weimar representatives, the treaty was met with violent nationalistic reaction and condemned by all sections of German society. Press organs of the rightist parties heaped scorn on democracy, and members of the Weimar government were held responsible for the humiliating state in which Germany found herself.[25] The German delegates who made the trip to Versailles to sign the treaty stated that they did so under duress and recognized no moral obligation to adhere to it. It was a tactical necessity, no more, and

Early National Socialism in America

evasion was to become a mark of patriotism. In a communique to Berlin, the leader of the German peace delegation, Mathias Erzberger, prophetically noted, "The German nation, which for fifty months has defied a world of enemies, will preserve in spite of every kind of violence, its liberty and unity. A nation of seventy million suffers but does not die."[26]

Germany did indeed suffer, and she did not die. Versailles neither stripped Germany of her power nor reintegrated her; rather Germany was pilloried. The early 1920s were years of extreme economic and social hardship. The population suffered as currencies collapsed and savings evaporated, influenza epidemics raged through the countryside, incidences of tuberculosis increased, undernourishment was common, and people starved. But, relative stability did prevail, and by

1928 Germany enjoyed the greatest degree of prosperity she had known during the decade. Tragically, as Germany moved toward repair and regrowth, the Great Depression hit Europe. The social fabric of the nation, already torn by war, defeat, and deprivation, now faced severe depression. The crash on Wall Street in the United States had brutal repercussions all over Europe, and in Germany the economy foundered. The economic catastrophe affected the tenuous political structure and opened the door to the already entrenched right. Weimar, established to appease the victorious Allies and hopefully to provide a shield against Bolshevism, could not stand the added strain that massive economic hardship added to its already shaky foundation. Parties of the left and right gained strength as the voting populace abandoned the incapable center. Fearful lest the quickly-growing left take power, President Hindenburg gravitated to the right in an effort to appease the public outcry for recovery and recapture the old social order.

The movement to the right that followed was not particular to Germany. During the twenty years of uneasy peace that followed World War I, popular dictatorships sprang up all over Europe. As one such phenomenon, Fascism flourished particularly in countries suffering from the degradation of defeat and severe economic depression, and threatened with the loss of status or impoverishment. National Socialism, Germany's form of Fascism, began as a protest movement by those who refused to accept either defeat or the post-war government. Although it was a product of the same social forces that gave rise to socialism and communism elsewhere, it reflected specific authoritarian and racial trends particular to German thinking.[27] Germany's National Socialist party reflected the prejudices, ambition, and personality of its leader, Adolf Hitler.[28]

In 1920, discharged from the army, Hitler joined the National Socialist German Workers' Party (NSDAP) and became its chief propagandist. As he moved to take over this tiny party, his obsessions became the four main points of the party's program: self-determination for all men of German blood, annulment of the Treaties of Versailles and St. Germain, living space for Germany's population, and the exclusion of Jews from society.

After an unsuccessful and premature bid for power in 1923 followed by a prison term, Hitler revised his tactics to enable him to work within the system. The years 1925-29 saw the growth and consolidation of the movement; the Party gained ground and had representatives elected to the Reichstag in 1928. The National Socialist vote rose steadily in state elections, and by 1930 it had become the second largest political party, though it contained far less than a majority of the population. In January 1933, after gaining thirty-seven percent of the total vote in the 1932 presidential elections, Hitler was appointed chancellor under the old and uncertain Hindenburg.

In the March 1933 general election, 43.9 percent of the population supported the National Socialist party and its lawless and harsh approach to government. The majority of the people readily adjusted themselves to Hitler's dictatorship. The National Socialists produced a national revival similar to the call of the Kaiser prior to World War I. Hitler offered the Germany people both a cause and a leader. He gave them tangible results that people could see and relate to: a revived economy and a new pride in themselves as Germans. Stimulating private industry, encouraging consumer

spending, and sponsoring massive public works programs, Hitler's government waged total war on unemployment with spectacular results. The people were
willing to support this new government that gave them
work and hope for their future. The mass reaction is
perhaps best exemplified by a popular poem of the
time, the "Song of the SA Man:"

> My belly rumbled with hunger,
> I fainted and went to bed,
> Then I heard in my ears a shouting—
> "Germany, awake!" it said.
> And I saw so many marching
> To the Third Reich, they cried;
> I had nothing to lose and nowhere to go,
> So I joined them and marched beside.[29]

These Germans who left Germany in the 1930s for
the United States left a phoenix rising from the ashes
of war and depression. They had experienced the
accomplishment of economic recovery and national
pride and related the positive aspects of the New Germany to their German American relatives and friends
to whom they were socially and culturally bound. In
the United States, the Depression lingered on. Recovery was in no way as dramatic or flamboyant as was
change in the New Germany under Hitler. The transfer
and exchange of ideas from German nationals to
American Germans who had suffered their own hard
times was a natural course of events. In the more radical of such German-American connections, such conversations often led to comparisons of the two countries and begged the question, "If Hitler's methods
could transform Germany, what could they do in the
United States?"

By 1930 seven million people of German descent
lived within the United States which had a total popu-

lation of 124 million. Of these, by 1933, approximately 600,000 were German-born.[30] Roughly 430,000 had arrived in the United States between 1919 and 1933.[31] Most of these immigrants, differing from their ancestors who had arrived earlier, were members of the recently industrialized middle class seeking security and opportunity. Alienated by civil strife, inflation, and general hard times in Germany, these embittered proletarians of the middle class sought a better life. Most came to settle permanently; some, however, merely wished to consolidate their future and return home.

Once in the United States, these immigrants sought out their own. In fact, German American organizations, both social and political, had been in functional existence since before World War I. In New York alone, the United German Societies comprised seventy organizations with more than 10,000 members. Typical German American organizations abounded in New York's predominantly German-speaking Yorkville section, a fifty-square block area in Manhattan. Clustered with dance- and beer-halls, the area offered cultural solidarity to an immigrant people who would often gather to bemoan the fate of Germany and German America. Significant within this population was the belief that Germany had been tricked into defeat. Indeed, the chief difference between those who formed groups in the 1920s and the 1930s, and those who had done so earlier, was that the new arrivals had witnessed Germany's defeat and had been profoundly affected by it. They had experienced the gross societal instability, economic hardships, and political factionalism in their homeland and brought this legacy with them.

Illustrative of the separatism and political thought

advocated by some German nationals, and crucial to the development of the German American Bund, was the formation of the National Socialist Teutonia Association in October 1924. Organized in Detroit by Fritz and Peter Gissibl, Alfred Ex, and Frank von Friedersdorff, Teutonia was the first National Socialist organization set up in the United States. Fritz Gissibl and the other founders of Teutonia were young zealots, members of the lost generation of Germany. Firmly committed to the evolving National Socialist ideology, they formed the group as a temporary organization to house displaced Party members.[32] The majority of these National Socialist compatriots were merely biding their time, awaiting their eventual return to the Fatherland. In the meantime, Teutonia's mission was to transplant the National Socialist ideology to newly-arrived German nationals living in the United States.[33]

Although Teutonia never gained recognition as the official American branch of the NSDAP, the organization was nevertheless fairly active.[34] It published a party newspaper, the *Vorposten*, as well as numerous handbills and pamphlets; collected and sent money to the NSDAP in Munich; and recruited quite a following from the German immigrant community. It is estimated, from statements made in letters by former members, that membership was a little over five hundred.[35] The social and economic climate of such cities as Detroit was as much responsible for this group's attraction as was any appeal of National Socialism. The heart of the newly emerging automotive industry, Detroit was experiencing rapid industrialization and mass production with resulting temporary unemployment as machines replaced manual labor. These centers of industrialization beckoned newly arrived immigrants only to dismiss them as mass productive techniques took hold. Those who fell prey to such experiences were usually more than open to the alternatives advocated by Teutonia. In 1932 the group had branches in Chicago, Los Angeles, New York City, and Cincinnati, and growth accelerated as the Depression deepened.

Before Hitler consolidated his power in Germany, Teutonia, and other National Socialist Germanic cells, lacked cohesion and credibility. The NSDAP in Germany was not strong enough to direct any activity outside the Reich, and support for the various groups inside the United States was small and predominantly local in nature. Indeed, many members of the NSDAP living in the United States preferred to congregate in disorganized cells and never joined Teutonia or made any effort to pool their potential power. This can be explained in part by the premise that most all of the groups did not consider the United States a fit home for National Socialism. Most of them, Teutonia included, were content to go about their business in relative isolation while they awaited the call home. As the NSDAP in their homeland grew stronger, chaos engulfed the American National Socialist enclaves as each group scrambled for the official National Socialist stamp of approval.

In 1931, an unofficial New York City cell of the NSDAP accomplished what Teutonia, and a host of others, could not. The National Socialist German Workers' Party, New York unit, or simply Gau-USA, was named the official standard-bearer of National Socialism in America. This move, by the NSDAP's newly created Foreign Section, threw Teutonia into a state of confusion. Although Gissibl had presented Teutonia as the genuine National Socialist organization in the United States, other Party members had been quick to point out that Teutonia's membership was basically composed of non-Party people. And whether or not that particular consideration affected the politics that determined the final outcome, it spelled death for Teutonia.

With the goal of assuming the leadership of the organization chosen by Germany to represent National Socialism in the United States, Gissibl declared Teutonia defunct and urged his membership to follow him into the Gau-USA. Gissibl and an equally zealous and more aggressive compatriot, Heinz Spanknoebel, assumed the leadership of branches of the Gau in Chicago and Detroit, areas where they had been previously active. With Gissibl and Spanknoebel thus in place, the stage was set for the evolution of the German American Bund.

ENDNOTES
Chapter 1

1. Many histories of the 1920s center around this theme. Some prominent works include Burl Noggle, *Into the Twenties: The United States from Armistice to Normalcy* (Chicago: University of Illinois Press, 1974); David M. Kennedy, *Over Here: The First World War and American Society* (New York: Oxford University Press, 1980); and *Frederick Lewis Allen, Only Yesterday: An Informal History of the 1920s* (Norwood, Pa.: Telegraph Books, 1931).

2. For casualty figures broken down by state, see James L. Stokesbury, *A Short History of World War I* (New York: William Morrow and Company, Inc., 1981), pp. 309-310.

3. For U.S. military participation in World War I see Edward M. Coffman, *The War to End All Wars: The American Military Experience in World War I* (New York: Oxford University Press, 1968); Peter Maslowski and Allan R. Millett, *For the Common Defense: A Military History of the United States of America* (New York: The Free Press, 1984), pp. 299-360; and Russell F. Weigley, *History of the United States Army* (New York: The Macmillan Company, 1967), pp. 342-394.

4. Excellent histories of the 1920s not already mentioned include Arthur Schlesinger, Jr., *The Crisis of the Old Order, 1919-1933* (Boston: Houghton Mifflin Company, 1957); William E. Leuchtenburg, *The Perils of Prosperity, 1914-1933* (Chicago: University of Chicago Press, 1958); and Geoffrey Perrett, *America in the Twenties* (New York: Simon and Schuster, 1982).

5. This has been a common perception among historians. For instance, see John Maynard Keynes, *The Economic Consequences of the Peace* (New York: Harcourt, Brace and Howe, 1920). Also see David Kennedy, *Over Here*; William

Leuchtenburg, *The Perils of Prosperity*; and Geoffrey Perrett, *America in the Twenties*.

6. Urbanization, of course, varied by region and far antedated World War I. In 1920, however, despite rapid urbanization, the United States was still an agricultural nation. Farming was by far her biggest business. See Gilbert C. Fite, *American Farmers: The New Minority* (Bloomington: Indiana University Press, 1981).

7. Irving Bernstein, *A History of the American Worker 1920-1933* (Baltimore Penguin Books, 1960), pp. 58-59.

8. Ibid., p. 64.

9. Geoffrey Perrett, *America in the Twenties*, p. 49. For an overview of the American labor movement see Melvyn Dubofsky, *Industrialism and the American Worker 1865-1920* (Arlington Heights, Ill.: Harlan Davidson, Inc., 1975); and Irving Bernstein, *A History of the American Worker 1920-1933*.

10. Racial tensions had been fired by problems associated with blacks in the armed forces. Blacks fought dutifully for the concept of democracy in which they had no voice. See Florette Henri, *Bitter Victory: A history of Black Soldiers in World War I* (New York: Doubleday and Company, Inc., 1970); and Emmett Jay Scott, *Scott's Official History of the American Negro in the World War* (New York: Arno Press and the *New York Times*, 1969).

11. For the Klan as a native-born, Protestant, rural movement pitted against Catholic, immigrant, urban America see Andre Siegfried, *America Comes of Age* (New York: Da Capo Press, Inc., 1927). See also John Moffat Mecklin, *The Ku Klux Klan: A Study of the American Mind* (New York: Russell and Russell, 1924); and David M. Chalmers, *Hooded Americanism: The History of the Ku Klux Klan* (Danbury, Conn.: Watts, Franklin, Inc., 1965).

12. Excellent works on the history of these groups are David A. Shannon, *The Socialist Party of America* (New York: Quadrangle Books, Inc. 1955); Daniel Bell, *Marxian Socialism in the United States* (Princeton: Princeton University Press, 1967); Frank A. Warren, *An Alternative Vision: The*

Socialist Party in the 1930s (Bloomington: Indiana University Press, 1974); Theodore Draper, *The Roots of American Communism* (New York: Hippocrene Books, Inc., 1957); and Harvey K. Klehr, *The Heyday of American Communism: The Depression Decade* (New York: Basic Books, 1985).

13. Far from working solely for the protection of veterans, the American Legion was heavily involved with politics, to included participation in a plot, financed by the American Liberty League, to overthrow Franklin Roosevelt in the 1930s. See Jules Archer, *The Plot to Seize the White House* (New York: Hawthorn Books, Inc., 1973).

14. This is not meant to indicate a causal relationship between the October crash and the Depression. Most historians now agree that they were not unrelated, but the Depression was not caused by the Crash. See John Kenneth Galbraith, *The Great Crash: 1929* (New York: Time Incorporated, 1954); and Robert Sobel, *The Great Bull Market: Wall Street in the 1920s* (New York: W. W. Norton and Company, Inc., 1968).

15. Works abound on the Great Depression. Excellent personal vignettes make up David A. Shannon's, *The Great Depression* (New Jersey: Prentice-Hall, Inc., 1960); and Studs Terkel's *Hard Times: An Oral History of the Great Depression* (New York: Pantheon Books, 1970). See also Arthur M. Schleslinger, Jr., *The Age of Roosevelt: The Coming of the New Deal* (Boston: Houghton Mifflin Company, 1959); William E. Leuchtenburg, *Franklin Delano Roosevelt and the New Deal, 1932-1940* (New York: Harper and Row, 1963); and Albert U. Romasco, *The Poverty of Abundance: Hoover, the Nation, and the Depression* (New York: Oxford University Press, 1965).

16. Alan Bullock, as quoted in Otto Friedrich, *Before the Deluge* (New York: Avon, 1973), pp. 126-127.

17. The Hoover-Roosevelt controversy has produced a mass of scholarly literature comparing personalities, policies, and effectiveness. See, for example, Joan Hoff Wilson, *Herbert Hoover: Forgotten Progressive* (Boston: Little, Brown and Company, 1975); Albert Romasco, *The Poverty of Abundance*; Frank Freidel, *Franklin Delano Roosevelt: Launch-*

ing the New Deal (Boston: Little, Brown, and Company, 1973); Paul Conkin, *The New Deal* (Arlington Heights, Ill.: Harlan Davidson, Inc., 1975); and James MacGregor Burns, *Roosevelt: The Lion and the Fox* (New York: Harcourt, Brace and World, Inc., 1956).

18. Literature on the Roosevelt Revolution includes James Burns, *Roosevelt: The Lion and the Fox*; William E. Leuchtenburg (ed.), *Franklin D. Roosevelt* (New York: Hill and Wang, 1967); and John G. Stoessinger, *Crusaders and Pragmatists: Movers of Modern American Foreign Policy* (New York: W. W. Norton and Company, 1979), pp. 35-53.

19. Most of the above-mentioned books touch on the controversiality of Roosevelt's New Deal. The debate centers on the question of whether Roosevelt's programs were part of a specific plan devised to break the Depression, extensions of Hooverian doctrine, or pragmatically applied band-aids.

20. There is no one work that adequately covers this radical upsurge. Good, specific works include Alan Brinkley, *Voices of Protest* (New York: Vintage Books, 1982); Richard Pells, *Radical Visions and American Dreams: Culture and Social Thought in the Depression Years* (Middletown, Conn.: Wesleyan University Press, 1977); Raymond Gram Swing, *Forerunners of American Fascism* (New York: Books for Libraries Press, 1935); John Carlson, *Under Cover* (New York: E. P. Dutton and Co., Inc., 1943); Roger Daniels, *The Bonus March: An Episode of the Great Depression* (Westport, Conn.: Greenwood, 1971); and George Wolkskill, *The Revolt of the Conservatives: History of the American Liberty League, 1934-1940* (Westport, Conn.: Greenwood, 1974); to name but a few.

21. Excellent works on the effects of World War I on Germany include Otto Friedrich, *Before the Deluge*; and D. J. Goodspeed, *The German Wars 1914-1945* (Boston: Houghton Mifflin Company, 1977), pp. 267-281.

22. See Ralph Haswell Lutz, *The German Revolution 1918-1919* (New York: AMS Press, 1968).

23. Gordon A. Craig and Hajo Holborn (ed.), *The Diplomats 1919-1939* (New Jersey: Princeton University Press, 1953), p. 145.

24. For a detailed breakdown on Germany's losses as a result of the Versailles Treaty and their subsequent effects see Stephen H. Roberts, *The House that Hitler Built* (New York: Harper and Brothers, Publishers, 1938). An annotated version of the treaty is *The Treaty of Versailles and After: Annotations of the Text of the Treaty* (New York: Greenwood Press, 1968).

25. The German government idealized the German cause throughout World War I. All efforts were made to place responsibility for the war on Germany's enemies. For a discussion of German war aims, to include political and social strategy, see L. L. Farrar, Jr., *The Short War Illusion* (Santa Barbara: Clio Press, 1973).

26. As found in Pierce G. Fredericks, *The Great Adventure: America in the First World War* (New York: E. P. Dutton and Co., Inc., 1960), p. 237.

27. The roots of German National Socialism are as illusive as is an adequate definition of that ideology. The best explanations are found in Peter Viereck, *Metapolitics from the Romantics to Hitler* (New York: Alfred A. Knopf, 1941); and Norman Rich, *Hitler's War Aims: Ideology, the Nazi State, and the Course of Expansion* (New York: W. W. Norton and Company, Inc., 1973).

28. One of the better biographies of Adolf Hitler is the massive work by Joachim C. Fest, *Hitler: A Biography* (New York: Harcourt Brace Jovanovich, Inc., 1973).

29. Poem by Bertolt Brecht as found in A. J. Ryder, *Twentieth Century Germany: From Bismarck to Brandt* (New York: Columbia University Press, 1973), pp. 309-310.

30. Richard O'Connor, *The German-Americans* (Boston: Little, Brown and Company, 1968), p. 437.

31. *The Statistical History of the United States from Colonial Times to the Present* (Stamford, Conn.: Fairfield, 1965), Series C 88-114, p. 56-57.

32. Gissibl himself was not a member of the NSDAP until 1930. "Card-carrying" membership at this stage of National Socialist organization was not imperative; Hitler's Nazification process had not yet begun.

33. For a review of Teutonia, see Sander A. Diamond, *The Nazi Movement in the United States 1924-1941* (Ithaca: Cornell University Press, 1974), pp. 91-99.

34. These organizations, from Teutonia through the German American Bund, would fight tooth and nail for the official NSDAP stamp. As will be seen, they often did so at the expense of their livelihood.

35. Sander Diamond, *The Nazi Movement in the United States*, p. 95.

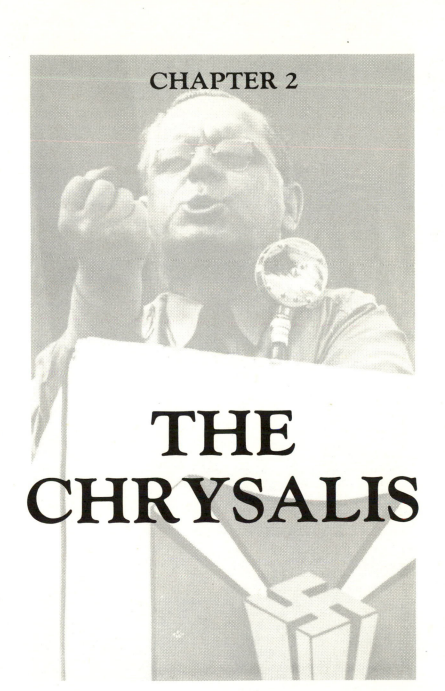

CHAPTER 2

THE
CHRYSALIS

CHAPTER 2

THE CHRYSALIS

Like its many predecessors, the Bund embodied existing National Socialist revolutionary thought. It shared the driving motivation, ideology, purpose, and membership of the groups which had preceded it. In fact, it was an extension and a carbon copy of Heinz Spanknoebel's creation, the Friends of New Germany, formed in 1933. Although a much more potent outpouring of National Socialism, the Bund's history paralleled that of Friends'. Equally significant, Germany's dealings with, and effects on, the Friends predetermined the measure of the Bund's existence. To this end, an examination of the Friends of New Germany and its relationship with Hitler's Third Reich is crucial.

The Bund began in Heinz Spanknoebel's lofty dream of becoming the American *Fuehrer*. Spanknoebel, who had moved from his collapsing Teutonia to the Gau-USA in pursuit of a leadership position, worked vigorously within that organization to achieve his goal. The designation of the Gau-USA as the official carrier of National Socialism in the United States was of momentous import to those seeking a German-sponsored, American-based, outpost. Heretofore there was no cohesion within the movement. Spanknoebel and others within the National Socialist movement hoped that the inter-group bickering would cease with Hitler's rise to power and that his ascendancy would

facilitate the consolidation of a unified mass movement. But that was not to be. Rivalries only increased
as each group vied for eminence.[1]

This extreme factionalism and continual in-fighting
between the infant National Socialist groups, as they
struggled to win Hitler's recognition, generated unfavorable press coverage for all concerned. Laboring to
maintain cordial relations with the United States, the
German Foreign Section of the NSDAP opted to put an
end to this chaotic situation and ordered the Gau-USA
disbanded in April 1933.[2] The Foreign Section hoped to
minimize German responsibility for these threatening
and vocal nascent National Socialist groups.

Spanknoebel wasted no time in taking advantage of
the mass confusion which followed Germany's decision to withdraw support from the Gau. Obsessed with
the goal of leading the United States to National
Socialism, he journeyed to Germany to seek command
approval for his dream. It worked. Spanknoebel
bluffed his way into the immature NSDAP infrastructure and bragged to Rudolf Hess, Deputy *Fuehrer*, that
he represented the will of thousands of German Americans.[3] Hess, willing to risk Germany's tenuous diplomatic position in order to secure what Spanknoebel
presented as an assured National Socialist outpost,
bought the story. Spanknoebel returned to the United
States with a document authorizing him to form a new
group. In July 1933, he set up temporary headquarters
in Yorkville, New York's predominantly Germanic section, and announced the formation of the Friends of
New Germany (*Bund der Freunde des neuen Deutschland*).[4] He was finally a *Fuehrer*.

Later that month, at the opening of their first
national convention in Chicago, Spanknoebel declared
that the National Socialist movement in the United

States had begun. Armed with Hess' personal authority, he was able to present the organization, and his appointment as leader, as the will of *Der Fuehrer*. He was successful; most Party and non-Party members accepted his leadership. Attracting members with the lure of racial exclusiveness and the promise of an invigorated German America, capitalizing on the economic hardships brought on by the Great Depression, and drawing on the very real fear of anti-German sentiment, membership in the Friends of New Germany rose steadily. With a substantial nucleus of German nationals surrounded by naturalized Germans and native-born Americans of German descent, membership, between 1933-1935, hovered between five and six thousand.[5]

The Friends of New Germany was a mirror image of Hitler's NSDAP inorganization, administration, and activity, from the leadership principle to the formation of a uniformed contingent, the OD (*Ordnungs-Dienst*), the counterpart to Hitler's SA.[6] Its most active years extended until 1935 and were spent fervently, and often recklessly, crusading the National Socialist cause. Upon assuming leadership of the group, Spanknoebel traveled across the United States delivering speeches denouncing racial amalgamation and international communism and exhorted his audiences to join in his fight to "clean up" America. Campaigning in predominantly Germanic communities, he urged his supporters to unite and fight for the preservation of their Germanic heritage.

Extremely militaristic and vehemently anti-Semitic, the Friends of New Germany attracted almost instant adverse attention. In his zeal to recreate the NSDAP in America, Spanknoebel gave little thought to the reactions of his adopted country. Stories circulated of

Leaflet promoting the Friends of New Germany

52

attacks on Jewish merchants of Nazi vandals painting swastikas on synagogues. During one anti-Semitic rally held in Newark, the OD, formed to crush internal opposition, abruptly ended the meeting by provoking a bloody brawl with the crowd. These antics only further alarmed a public already concerned over motion picture portrayals of marching, uniformed columns of Nazis.[7] Germany, aware of the public furor created by Spanknoebel's activities, ordered him "to refrain from any activity until further notice."[8] The caveat went unheeded.

America, noting the growing Nazi menace in Germany and mindful of World War I experiences with German fifth columns, real and imagined, demanded the early policing of the movement. In October 1933, Congressman Samuel Dickstein, chairman of the House Committee on Immigration and Naturalization, requested the deportation of Spanknoebel on the grounds that he had failed to register with the State Department as an agent of a foreign government. Spanknoebel hastily left the United States before he could be apprehended, but his activities and the direction he had set for the Friends of New Germany coalesced burgeoning American fears of foreign infiltration and sabotage and initiated further investigations.[9] A New York grand jury indicated it intended to investigate the Friends, and Dickstein began work on a resolution authorizing a Congressional examination.[12]

Meanwhile, Spanknoebel's hasty departure, and the Congressional attention that the "Spanknoebel Affair" had generated, threw the Friends of New Germany into a state of turmoil. Intraparty revolts and splinter movements sprang up while the leadership fought over the question of succession. After considerable dispute, Fritz Gissibl, Spanknoebel's long time compatriot and trusty Party stalwart, was named *Bundesleiter* of the Friends, and, in an effort to thwart Dickstein's impending Congressional investigation, adopted a move to "Americanize" the Friends.[11] To give the impression of a disassociation with Germany, the NSDAP dropped Gissibl's name from its membership lists (however, he maintained a clandestine position in the Party), and the new *Bundesleiter* began naturalization proceedings. The hope was that Germany would no longer be held accountable for Gissibl's, and consequently the Friends', actions.

Despite the chaos created by the leadership change and the adoption of this "Americanization," the Friends of New Germany experienced a period of growth and expansion. Away from national headquarters, where turmoil reigned, the movement stabilized and units were formed in a dozen additional cities, while aims and ideology for the group were established and strengthened.[12] Temporarily subduing their pro-German, anti-democratic stance, the Friends concentrated on an important local economic issue to solidify their political base. American Jewry, concerned with National Socialism's ominous anti-Semitism, had organized a counter-boycott of German goods to retaliate against the boycott of Jewish businesses in Germany and had urged their fellow Americans to support them.[13] Proclaiming itself a defensive movement organized by concerned German nationals to protect themselves from this perceived Jewish-Bolshevik menace, the Friends of New Germany actively moved to counter the Jewish boycott of German goods. The Friends, thus presenting themselves as the protectors of American-German business, monitored trade to ostracize Jewish merchants. They thereby streng-

thened their control and exacerbated existing anti-
Semitism in their neighborhood communities.

Once established in these segregated and easily
monitored communities, the Friends resumed their
ideological attack. In accordance with the dictates of
National Socialism, the group's mission was to make
all Americans of German descent aware of their Germanness in order to amplify feelings of obligation to
Germany. This was accomplished relatively easily as
the susceptible Germanic population tended to congregate in tight-knit communities for reasons of convenience, culture, and safety. To further the process of
Americanization, the Friends altered the basic tenets
of National Socialism to fit their new base in the
United States. Anti-black sentiment was added to the
anti-Semitic and anti-Communist stance, and these
became as essential and as virulent within the American faction as they were within the Reich. Drawing on
Hitler's view of the United States as a weak-willed,
racially degenerate country, the Friends cried that it
was the superior Aryan who was destined to cleanse
and reinvigorate the United States.[14]

While the Friends of New Germany demanded and
received absolute obedience from their membership,
the group hardly received anything akin to acceptance
from the general American public. Because they were
very active and extremely vocal, the Friends of New
Germany were seldom out of the limelight. Parading in
brownshirt look-alike uniforms in New York, publishing widely circulated National Socialist tracts in Philadelphia, Detroit, Chicago, and Cincinnati, parroting
all for the NSDAP's proposals and heartily defending
Germany and her actions, the Friends created an
image that could not be reconciled even to a public
raised on the first Amendment. Their image was

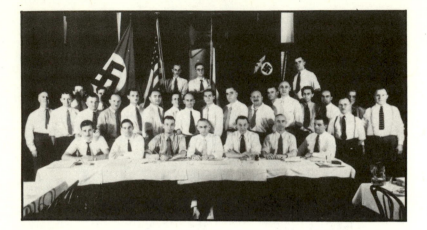

Friends of the New Germany, circa 1935
(Fritz Kuhn is 9th from right)

further tarnished by the increasingly numerous reports from Germany about the persecution of Jews, the increased militarization of German life, attacks on Christian churches, and violent Party purges.

Indicative of the public mood, on 7 March 1934, some 20,000 people gathered at Madison Square Garden to witness a mock trial sponsored by the American Federation of Labor and the American Jewish Congress heralded as *Civilization v. Hitler*.[15] Fear of the Nazi fifth column now coalesced. Germany's aggressiveness, and that of her sister movement in America, became apparent to all—from the Jewish grocer attempting to eke out a living in Yorkville under the Friends' martial watch all the way up to the President of the United States.[16]

Nor did America's reaction go unnoticed in Germany. Diplomatically precariously perched at this particular juncture in her statehood, Germany struggled to assume a less threatening stance in her foreign relations. Desperately needing worldwide recognition and peaceful trade relations, in order to solidify her power base for future expansion, she initiated a propaganda campaign to make National Socialism more palatable to the United States. She claimed that National Socialism was not for export and disavowed responsibility for National Socialist groups in the United States. Owing to the multiplicity of her foreign policy apparatus, this effort, for the most part, only confused and further complicated relations.

Although diplomatic channels had long been in functional existence, Hitler's personal beliefs, in combination with the power held by the state-supported NSDAP, pitted one foreign policy agency against another; as a result conflicting policies often emanated from the same agency. Historically, orthodox channels of intergovernmental diplomacy were covered by the German Foreign Office. However, Hitler's belief that, on the whole, diplomats were unrealistic, led to a general bypassing of traditional diplomatic channels and a growth of rival agencies.[17] In the course of 1934, propaganda and subversive work outside the Reich were taken over and conducted by the NSDAP through such agencies as the *Auslands-Organisation* (AO), the Party's Foreign Policy Office (*Aussenpolitisches Amt*, or APA), the German Foreign Institute (*Deutsches Auslands-Institut*, or DAI), and the League of Germans Abroad (*Verein fuer das Deutschtum im Ausland*, or VDA).[18]

By far the most aggressive of the agencies dealing with German nationals abroad was the AO under *Gauleiter* Ernst Wilhelm-Bohle, himself a foreign-born German and protege of Rudolf Hess. Formed in 1931, the AO's official mission was to coordinate the work of Party members in foreign countries and to establish and expand Party groups abroad. The AO held total control over relations between Party agencies in Germany and the foreign groups.[19]

Equally important to the direction and organization of foreign German nationals was the powerful VDA, perhaps the bitterest rival of the AO, which since 1880 had devoted its efforts to the preservation of schools, cultural organizations, and political activities of ethnic Germans throughout the world. At first an independent agency, after 1933 the VDA was brought under the Party wing, eventually put under the auspices of the SS, and became the conduit for National Socialist ethnic policies and propaganda.

In the case of the United States, these separate pathways of policy implementation intersected at the consulates, which, like most other governmental bodies in Germany, were undergoing Nazification. Nazification, it must be remembered, did not occur spontaneously with Hitler's assumption of power. Rather, government agencies were gradually infiltrated, some taking longer than others, depending on their relative importance to the running of the state. The foreign ministry was especially slow to become NSDAP-controlled. German diplomatic emissaries in foreign countries often held their posts without Party membership because of their expertise in their particular area. The extent of Party affiliation among diplomats, therefore, often depended on their usefulness to Berlin. The German Ambassador to the United States, for instance, remained far more aloof from Party control than did the less experienced and more numerous area consuls. This posed a serious problem. Because American National Socialist groups tended to gravitate toward the German consuls as their unofficial representatives of German culture, and since the consuls were generally at least Party-approved and not always in sympathy with the Foreign Office, diplomatic communication between the United States and Germany was often jumbled and confused.

Moreover, the above-mentioned agencies posed a particular problem to foreign governments as well as their own. Nations dealing with the New Germany considered policies and practices of any one of them the result of deliberate planning of Hitler or his immediate advisors. Although not necessarily the case, this furthered the belief that Germany's foreign policy emanated from a single, unified body and was therefore representative of German foreign planning. Nor was the German hierarchy unaffected by the maneuverings of its various foreign policy agencies. Interference among the agencies was common, detracting from the efficiency of all, and their simple existence undermined the authority of the Foreign Office.

The situation was further aggravated by the fact that while National Socialist groups outside the Reich viewed their work as crucial to the survival of the New Germany, this feeling was not universally held by the members of the high command.[20] The utility and extent of fifth column activity was constantly debated among various agencies despite the fact that it was more than likely never a topic of overall primary concern. For instance, although Hess had given Spanknoebel the authority to form the Friends of New Germany, Hitler may not have known or approved of Hess' action. Historical debate may never exhaust the question of Hitler's involvement in the day-to-day functioning of the Third Reich; in the diplomatic arena it matters little as contemporary perceptions were what formulated the reality under which governments worked. As Germany presented herself as a complete entity, and since for the most part she made no refer-

ence to the personalities or agencies other than Hitler
and the NSDAP, it seemed only natural and logical to
accept the image projected.

To this end, the world simply accepted Germany's
militaristic stance and hardline propaganda. Germany's cry for the organization and deification of the
Aryan race affected not only the German government
and its people, but all others as well. The logic behind
this driving propaganda was simple and permeated all
aspects of the culture. To the National Socialist, organization of all Germans was crucial to their racial heritage. In the early 1930s, the large German communities
residing outside the Reich were seen as potential reser-
voirs of German culture, which, if preserved, could be
tapped, should the struggle demand it. By 1930,
approximately thirty million Germans lived outside
the Reich—both German citizens (*Reichsdeutsche*) and
those of German descent who were citizens of foreign
countries (*Volksdeutsche*).[21] All were considered equal
members of the German racial elite, and the official
program of the Party made little distinction between
the two. Blood and race tied all Germans to a common
destiny under Hitler. Not only was this the claim to
legitimacy put forth by the Friends of New Germany
and later the German American Bund, but it was also
the key to Hitler's drive for Germanic supremacy and
the cornerstone of propaganda emanating from the
Reich.

The United States, then, responded to German propaganda by assuming that the German government
was a monolithic body, and that German nationals
residing outside the Third Reich represented the German government. The United States paid scant attention to the frenzied German rebuttals to the contrary.[22]
The American suspicion of a National Socialist fifth

Hitler's Birthday rally leaflet

column was instead fueled by the aggressive stance of the AO and the VDA and further encouraged by Hitler's bombastic calls for a worldwide National Socialist revolution. The Friends of New Germany parroted this perceptually subversive preaching, thereby placing themselves in jeopardy.

The United States was not about to let this movement go unchecked. In April 1934, the Dickstein-McCormack Congressional Investigatory Committee began its examination of the Friends of New Germany. Ignoring the claim of Congressman Terry M. Carpenter of Nebraska that the investigation would only create racial prejudice, Congress passed a resolution authorizing the investigation of Nazi activities in the United States by a vote of 168-31 in January 1934.[23] Although chaired by John McCormack of Massachusetts, the Committee was the brainchild of its cochairman, Samuel Dickstein.[24]

Generally, the investigations were conducted carefully and were relatively respectful of witnesses. The Committee met in executive session from April to July 1934, in an effort to protect the witnesses' reputations and civil rights. The few public hearings, during which time witnesses were allowed counsel, were conducted for the most part by Chairman McCormack who strove to keep the investigations at least orderly. Dickstein, however, raised the emotional ante by regularly taunting and baiting witnesses.[25] His inquisitorial passions were slaked by the fervent rebuttals, incongruously sprinkled with shouts of "Heil Hitler!" from supporters of subpoenaed German Americans.

The Committee's work drew wide support from a public obsessed with a growing passion over seditious behavior as the first concrete action to condemn National Socialist activities in the United States got underway. Americans turned on their radios and bought papers to receive detailed accounts of the hearings, and generally condoned the proceedings. The German American community recoiled; their language press labeled the Committee the "Jewish Inquisition," and Dickstein America's number one "German hater."[26]

Many German Americans called before the Committee were not only subjected to abuse on the witness stand but were treated with intolerance outside the hearing room as well. Although the Congressional investigation's purpose was not to prosecute known criminals but merely to investigate a political phenomenon, most called before the body were branded as guilty of "un-Americanism"—a term that would prove to be as all-encompassing as it was vague. The German American community was convinced that what was meant by un-American was being too pro-German; Representative Maury Maverick of Texas, staunch opponent of investigatory action, noted that, "Un-American is simply something that somebody else does not agree to."[27]

The Dickstein-McCormack Committee reported its findings in February 1935.[28] The heart of the report centered on the history of Nazi organizations in the United States.[29] Noting that, on the whole, most German Americans were unquestionably loyal United States citizens, the report maintained that the adverse publicity the Nazi groups had sustained as a result of the hearings, had halted their growth.

Indeed, the Dickstein-McCormack Committee had struck fear in the heart of German America. Memories of the fanatical anti-German sentiment that had swept the country during World War I were reinvigorated by this investigatory action. Far from debilitating the

National Socialist movement, however, the Committee's attacks only encouraged the group to fight for its
survival. Membership doubled from October 1934 to
March 1935 as the hunted banded together.[30]
Throughout early 1935 the Friends' activities seemed
only more flagrantly National Socialist. They actively
supported Bruno Hauptmann, a German-born carpenter, during his trial for the kidnapping and murder of
the Lindbergh baby, sponsored a dance to celebrate
Hitler's birthday, and conducted a mass rally in New
York where they adopted resolutions defending German armament and denouncing international
communism.

America's apprehension of these indigenous Nazis
not only fueled the German American's fear of persecution and mobilized the general public against the
threat of internal Nazism, but affected her already
strained relations with Germany as well. In light of the
Dickstein-McCormack furor, Germany decided to put
an end to her ties with the Friends of New Germany.
The group had been carefully monitored by various
NSDAP agencies since its inception, and its usefulness
had long been seriously disputed. Germany had, after
all, *not* authorized the Friends' activities, and Hitler's
office had given strict instructions that foreign groups
refrain from political activities in their host country.[31]
In October 1934, Hitler received the head of the Steuben
Society, one of German America's oldest and most conservative social coalitions, Mr. Theodore H. Hoffmann,
who expressed severe criticism of the Friends.[32] He told
an only mildly-interested Hitler that, "The activities
which they, as foreigners, engaged in in America, were
only harmful without benefitting Germany and
created disharmony in German-American circles."[33]
Germany moved in accordance with this view, and on

11 October 1935, the German Foreign Ministry and the AO ordered all German nationals, including those holding first papers, to resign from the Friends. Noncompliance with the order would result in the loss of German citizenship. As approximately sixty percent of the Friends' membership were German nationals, this move was meant to be an effective threat to the life of the organization.[34] In November, *Gauleiter* Bohle, in a communication to Hess, echoed Germany's concern when he advised, "Absolute passivity toward the U.S.A. . . . is based on my view that at the present time any overt efforts made in the United States and on the behalf of the New Germany are entirely pointless."[35]

Germany's disavowal of the Friends of New Germany precipitated chaos in the ranks. The belief was widespread that the October edict was the result of a

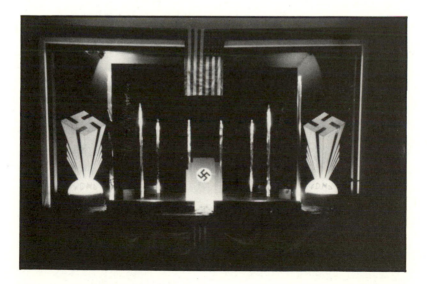

Friends of the New Germany, c. 1935

plot developed by members of the consular staff in America to undermine the movement, rather than a decision made by the high command to terminate the movement. Gissibl left for Berlin to plead for a reversal of the decision, but his arguments were in vain. Germany regarded maintenance of her position with the United States as far more important than the survival of a small, splintered outpost. On Christmas Day 1935, Hess reaffirmed the October edict in a letter released to the Associated Press.[36]

Far from solving the "German American problem" by speeding the collapse of the movement, the October edict prompted both consolidation and a change in course. The Friends of New Germany proceeded to change, chameleon-like, to suit the new demands made of it.

ENDNOTES
Chapter 2

1. Almost daily, throughout the spring and summer of 1933, newspapers in New York City carried stories of the inter-group fighting and internal chaos. For example, see the New York *Evening Journal* for this time period. See also Sander A. Diamond, *The Nazi Movement in the United States 1924-1941* (Ithaca: Cornell University Press, 1974), pp. 110-111.

2. Several factors combined from 1933 to 1941 to undermine US-German relations: differences involving trade, disarmament, international payments, as well as political ideologies. Ideological problems often proved the most pervading, seeping out into the public's view. As a result, for example, in May 1933, an anti-Nazi demonstration with 100,000 participants was held in New York City. For a diplomatic discussion of US-German relations during this period see Kenneth Paul Jones (ed.), *U. S. Diplomats in Europe 1919-1941* (Oxford: Clio Press, 1981), pp. 113-126.

3. Rudolf Hess, himself a foreign German born in Egypt, vigorously supported the recruitment of National Socialist members from abroad, and, as Deputy *Fuehrer*, took control and supervised all activities regarding the German element abroad. See U. S. Department of State, *Documents on German Foreign Policies, 1918-1945, from the Archives of the German Foreign Ministry*, Series C (Washington, D. C.: USGPO, 1949-1950), II: 49. Hereafter noted as DGFP.

4. A comprehensive history of the Friends of New Germany can be found in Sander Diamond, *The Nazi Movement in the United States*, pp. 128-178.

5. Ibid., p. 146.

6. The OD, originally organized as an adjunct of the Teutonia Association, was later carried over to the German American Bund.

7. President Roosevelt was himself concerned over such portrayals. See DGFP, C, I, p. 392.

8. As quoted in Donald M. McKale, *The Swastika Outside Germany* (Kent, Ohio: Kent State University Press, 1977), p. 71.

9. Spanknoebel returned to Germany a hero. He became one of Himmler's SS officers.

10. Excellent examinations of Congress' investigative activities are Walter Goodman's *The Committee* (New York: Farrar, Straus and Giroux, 1968): and August Raymond Ogden, *The Dies Committee: A Study of the Special House Committee for the Investigation of Un-American Activities, 1938-1944* (Washington, D. C.: The Catholic University of America Press, 1945.)

11. Initially Spanknoebel had designated Ignatz Griebl, an American physician, to succeed him. It was thought that an American citizen could quiet the discontent. Hess, despite the fact that he wanted to Americanize the movement, was unsure of his ability to control Griebl and instead passed the leadership to Gissibl. Gissibl would exert a powerful influence on the Friends throughout its existence, but was not continually in power. He was succeeded by Reinhold Walter and later Hubert Schnuch, both naturalized citizens. Although differing very slightly in politics, personal rivalries among them spent much of the Friends' energies, leaving it open to crises and to collapse.

12. The outline of the program can be found in *Das neue Deutschland—Was geht es uns an*? found in the Records of the National Socialist German Labor Party, Microcopy T-81/27/24732-41, National Archives, Washington, D. C.

13. See Samuel Untermeyer, *Nazis Against the World: The Counterboycott is the only Defense against Hitlerism's Threat to Civilization* (New York: 1934).

14. Hitler's conception of the United States has been a matter of debate for historians. Prior to 1928, Hitler wrote of the dynamism and potential of America in *Mein Kampf* (1925) and *Hitlers zweites Buch* L1928). During the Depression, however, Hitler's speeches and writings indicate only scorn.

See, for example, Hitler's speech to the Reichstag, 17 May 1933, in Norman H. Baynes (ed.), *The Speeches of Adolf Hitler, 1922-1939* (London: Oxford University Press, 1942), II: 1041; and Message from Hitler to Roosevelt, 14 March 1934, in DGFP, D, II, p. 611.

15. *New York Times*, 8 March 1934.

16. DGFP, C, I, p. 392.

17. See Saul Friedlander, *Prelude to Downfall: Hitler and the United States 1939-1941* (London: Chatto and Windus, 1967), ch. 1; and Karl Dietrich Bracher, *The German Dictatorship: The Origins, Structure, and Effects of National Socialism* (New York: Holt, Rinehart, and Winston, 1970), pp. 319-329.

18. These are merely the largest of the agencies which could have or did maintain some influence over the Friends of New Germany or later the German American Bund. Other agencies existed for dealing with German abroad and include: the *Dienststelle Ribbentrop*, the *Volksdeutsche Mittelstelle* (VoMi), and the central agency of Hitler's elite guard, the SS.

19. Extremely influential, the AO was given Cabinet status in 1937 with jurisdiction over all Germans in foreign countries. For an excellent study on the AO see Donald McKale, *The Swastika Outside Germany*.

20. Donald McKale, for example, in *The Swastika Outside Germany*, maintains that Hitler did not see fifth columns as serious mechanisms of foreign policy. In a communication from the State Secretary in the Reich Chancellory to the Foreign Minister, Hitler is credited with saying that while one could not prevent National Socialists abroad from meeting amongst themselves, he had given strict instructions that they were in all circumstances to refrain from political activities in the country which was their host. The memo goes on to indicate that Germany was *not* authorizing the Friends of New Germany's activities. DGFP, C, III, p. 1115-1116.

21. The most accurate approximations of the number of Germans residing outside the Reich are in Wilhelm Winkler, *Statistisches Handbuch fur das gesamte Deutschtum* (Berlin: *Verlag Deutsche Rundschau*, 1927), p. 25.

22. See, for example, DGFP, C, III, pp. 653-655; and DGFP, C, IV, pp. 23-27 and 381-383.

23. August Ogden, *The Dies Committee*, p. 33.

24. Walter Goodman, in *The Committee*, goes so far as to name Samuel Dickstein, veteran Congressman of twenty-two years, the Father of the Investigatory Committees.

25. See, for example, Walter Goodman, *The Committee*, pp. 10-11.

26. *Deutsche Zeitung*, 4 January and 14 April 1934.

27. Walter Goodman, *The Committee*, p. 27.

28. U. S. Congress, House, 74th Congress, 1st Session, Special Committee on Un-American Activities, *Investigation of Nazi and Other Propaganda* (Washington, D. C.: 1935).

29. Not to be confused with Roosevelt's CCC camps or youth organizations which were also uniformed.

30. Sander Diamond, *The Nazi Movement in the United States*, p. 168.

31. DGFP, C, III, pp. 1115-1116.

32. The Steuben Society was organized in May 1919 for the express purpose of changing the image of Germans and Germany that had developed during the war.

33. DGFP, C, III, pp. 1115-1116.

34. Sander Diamond, *The Nazi Movement in the United States*, pp. 191-192; Donald McKale, *The Swastika Outside Germany*, p. 91; Leland V. Bell, *In Hitler's Shadow: The Anatomy of American Nazism* (New York: Kennikat Press, 1973), p. 15.

35. DGFP, C, III, p. 1115-1116.

36. *New York Times*, 25 December 1935.

CHAPTER 3

THE
PHOENIX

CHAPTER 3

THE PHOENIX

Cheered by a crowd of 1,500 at the New York Turn-halle in April 1936, Fritz Julius Kuhn outlined his proposals for th newly organized German American Bund. Outfitted in the uniform of the Third Reich, Kuhn thundered his advocation of labor organizations, the Uniformed Service (OD), active youth groups, and American politics.

"Our task over here is to fight Jewish Marxism and Communism," proclaimed the newly appointed *Bundesfuehrer*.[1] In describing the Bund's purposes to the wildly applauding crowd, the "American *Fuehrer*" proposed the unification of German Americans into a politically conscious group in order to fight communism. "We cannot and must not deny our racial characteristics," declared Kuhn, "because if we did we would be useless to America."[2] So long as there's a swastika, there'll be no hammer and sickle in this country."[3]

So emerged the German American Bund—the direct successor of the Friends of New Germany. Officially the *raison d'etre* of the German American Bund was put forth, with no less melodrama, by Kuhn in his opening publication, *Awake and Act*. The Bund proposes, Kuhn declared:

> . . . purposes to take a positive attitude in the affairs of the country while complying unqualifiedly with its duties to the United

Anti-Semitic propaganda caricature

States. We shall educate the American people to become friends of the New Germany.

But for us, dear friends, there is no longer a new Germany—for us there is but the one and only Germany, the Germany of today—the National Socialist Germany—the Third Reich![4]

The Bund declares its allegiance:

. . . to honor and defend the Constitution, the flag and institutions of the United States of America; to combat all atheistic teachings and abuses of the pulpits; to oppose all racial intermixture between Aryans and Asiatics, Africans and other non-Aryans; to fight communism; to break up the dictatorship of the Jewish-international minority; to strive for a true peace; and to defend the right to cherish the German language and German customs.[5]

The pledge exemplifies the triadic nature of Bundist philosophy. In part, it is strongly American, but it is also vehemently National Socialist and liberally Germanic. The Bund had no trouble reconciling the inherent differences. National Socialism was the core doctrine, fueled by calls to unify Germandom with Americanism, applied as necessary for protection and public consumption. Moreover, the Bund proclaimed it was staunchly opposed to all "isms" including communism, Zionism, Nazism, and Fascism. It stridently maintained that it was neither officially nor financially supported by the National Socialist government of Germany.

Kuhn's appointment came at the time of Germany's call for the withdrawal of all German nationals from the Friends of New Germany. In an effort to save itself, or at least its principles, the Friends passed through a metamorphosis which resulted in a new leader and a new name. It became the *Amerikadeutscher Volksbund* (AV)—the German American People's League, shortened to the German American Bund—under Fritz Kuhn, a naturalized American citizen. These changes were intended to remove the obvious German stamp from the organization and illustrate its professed Americanism. Neither was clear, nor successful.

With Kuhn's appointment as national leader in 1936, the Bund assumed through him a new stance and personality. Under Kuhn's leadership the Bund achieved national notoriety and helped to coalesce the xenophobia that engulfed the United States during the war years and immediately thereafter. Although the Friends of New Germany had been influential enough to affect American-German relations, their activities had been viewed as an obvious German attempt to mobilize a fifth column in the United States. The

Friends never gained the membership or publicity to be viewed as anything more than a potentially dangerous foreign cancer. The German American Bund, however, as the Americanized version of the Friends, stressed its independence from Germany and became infinitely more threatening.

The name and leadership change notwithstanding, the German American Bund merely attempted to cloak its National Socialism in additional American trappings. However, structurally, the Bund was the Friends of New Germany. Organizational methods and administrative guidelines were transferred in toto from the Friends to the Bund. Most significant of these was the leadership principle or *Fuehrerprinzip*. Inherent to National Socialism, this concept of organization lent considerable strength to the leader or *Fuehrer* of the organization. Under the *Fuehrerprinzip* the national leader had supreme authority over all activities and aspects of the organization. Furthermore, all Bund members were required to pledge their acceptance of the *Fuehrerprinzip*, thus strengthening the leader's totalitarian control. Only the national convention, a body of delegates chosen from each state level that met annually to review policy, could depose the national leader. And since delegates were pyramidically chosen by the national *Fuehrer*, deposition was extremely unlikely. The German American Bund, in fact, was Fritz Kuhn. Although the AV is often characterized as an extension of Hitler's NSDAP, it was first and foremost an extension of Fritz Kuhn.

Kuhn was dubbed the American *Fuehrer* by the press and took on all of the satanic characteristics that were attributed to his mentor, Adolf Hitler. He was portrayed as an illiterate thug and general malcontent;

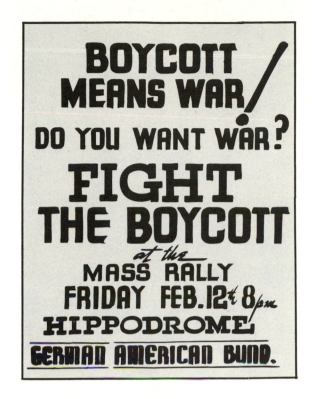

Advertisement for a Bund rally

newspaper accounts proclaimed him a Nazi, and he
was branded an obvious misfit in American society.[6]

Kuhn spent his formative years in Germany. He was
born in Munich in May 1896 and grew up in a middle
class family in the shadow of Kaiser Wilhelm. He
earned the Iron Cross defending the Fatherland in the
First World War as a lieutenant in the infantry. When
the war ended, and disillusion and unemployment
settled over Germany, Kuhn found solace and camaraderie in the Freikorps. By the time he was twenty-six
years old, Kuhn had experienced relative calm and

Fritz Kuhn in WWI Uniform

prosperity at home, the glory and horror of war, and the madness of post-war domestic chaos and violence. These were the conditions that spawned Germany's "lost generation" of the Weimar Republic—those unable to rise above the economic and social realities of a state in flux. Kuhn, however, was not lost. Driven by a dream, and provided with the opportunity to attain it, he augmented his tour in the Freikorps with studies at the University of Munich. There he studied chemical engineering and graduated with the equivalent of a master's degree in 1922. In 1923, he married Elsa Walthers and left a Germany devastated by war for Mexico. For five years he awaited entry into the United

States. During these years Kuhn worked as a lab chemist for the LaCorona Oil Company in Tampico, as a
chemist for the Marcisis Company, a cosmetic manu-
facturer in Mexico City from 1924-7, and as a teacher at
the College of Mexico City from 1927-1928.[7] He entered
the United States in 1928 and settled in Detroit like so
many other immigrants hopeful of employment with
the burgeoning automotive industry. Kuhn worked in

The Bund's uniform

A Member of the Women's Auxiliary

Detroit for eight years, first as a chemist at the Henry Ford Hospital and then with the Ford Motor Company. During this period, Kuhn, like many others, sought cultural comfort in the local German American fraternity and joined the Friends of New Germany. He assumed the leadership of the Detroit regional group of the Friends and, coincidentally, became a naturalized American citizen in 1934.[8] At the national convention of the Friends, held on 28-29 March 1936, in Buffalo, New York, Kuhn was elected president of the organization.[9] Presidency of the Friends assured him the same office when the organization regrouped in April. Upon being named national leader of the German American Bund, Kuhn gave up chemistry to devote his full time and attention to the Bund.

The new *Bundesfuehrer* was a large, imposing man, standing 5'11" and weighing slightly over 200 pounds, with a strong face framed by graying brown hair. He was forceful and decisive in character as well, armed with an aggressive personality and endowed with considerable force and intelligence.[12] Former Bund members have drawn a picture of an extremely professional, dedicated, and slightly distant man who inspired great admiration and trust. According to their recollections and Kuhn's writings, along with the histrionics and demagoguery lay a firm conviction of American strength and total allegiance to the United States.[11] In the eyes of most Americans, however, Kuhn epitomized all that was evil and dangerous about National Socialism. Upon undertaking leadership of the Bund he dropped the title of president, preferring instead the title of *Bundesfuehrer*. He proudly proclaimed to audiences in Madison Square Garden, the Yorkville Casino, and the German American Bund

Home in Union City, New Jersey, that National Socialist Germany pointed the way to America's future.
Lacking the personal magnetism of Adolf Hitler, Kuhn
nevertheless made use of sensationalism and the elan
of Fascism. Unlike his predecessors he created a cultic
organization. Kuhn spoke with a heavy German
accent, and his movement was bedecked in swastikas
and jackboots. As Kuhn pledged his support of Hitler,
Bundists pledged support of Kuhn. He was indeed the

Bundesfuehrer Fritz Kuhn

American *Fuehrer*. Under his guidance, the Bund became the aggressive arm of American Fascism.[12]

The Bund commanded its largest following in centers of significant German immigrant populations. Although the Bund was organized throughout the United States, the active enclaves were found primarily in the northeast United States due to immigration patterns and available employment. Affiliates in the midwest, southwest, and far west were not as vocal, nor did they attract the media coverage that the national center in the New York City-New Jersey areas did.

The Bund was divided into three regions, or *Gaue*— the East, Midwest, and West. The Eastern *Gau* operated out of the National Headquarters in the Yorkville section of New York City, and local branches included those in Albany, Astoria, the Bronx, Brooklyn, Buffalo, Glendale, Jamaica, Lindenhurst, Nassau County, New Rochelle, Manhattan, Poughkeepsie, Rochester, Rockland County, Schenectady, South Brooklyn, State Island, Syracuse, Troy, Utica, White Plains, and Yonkers in New York; Baltimore, Maryland; Washington, D. C.; Bergen County, Hudson County, Newark, Passaic County, and Trenton in New Jersey; Boston, Massachusetts; Bridgeport, Danbury, Greenwich, New Britain, New Haven, Norwalk, Stamford, and Waterbury in Connecticut; Providence, Rhode Island; Lancaster, Philadelphia, Pittsburgh, Reading, and Sellersville in Pennsylvania. The Midwestern *Gau* was centered in Chicago and included South Chicago, Illinois; Cincinnati, Cleveland, Dayton, and Toledo, Ohio; Detroit, Michigan; Fort Wayne, Gary, Hammond, Indianapolis, and South Bend, Indiana; Kenosha, Milwaukee, and Sheboygan, Wisconsin; Minneapolis and St. Paul, Minnesota; Omaha, Nebraska; St. Louis, Missouri; Taylor, Texas. The Western *Gau* was head-

A local New York unit of the Bund

quartered in Los Angeles and included Oakland, Concord, Petaluma, Santa Barbara, San Diego, San Francisco, and San Gabriel, California; Salt Lake City, Utah; Portland, Oregon; Seattle and Spokane, Washington.[13]

Application for membership was addressed in Article IV, Section 1 of the 1936 Bund Constitution:

> Membership in this Bund is primarily open to all Americans and prospective citizens of Aryan blood of German extraction and of good reputation. Membership may also be extended to other national elements filling requirements of our membership application.

Not surprisingly, an examination of available Bund membership lists reveals that the core of the organization consisted of recruits from the German American community.[14] While the Bund was directed almost exclusively by German nationals recently naturalized as American citizens, American-born Americans and German nationals were attracted as well. In order to open the organization to more participation, Kuhn bypassed Hess' edict of 1935, which outlawed German nationals from participation in the Friends and other similar groups, by creating the Prospective Citizens League in October 1936.[15] Members in the Prospective Citizens League were required to take out first papers towards naturalization and were prohibited from holding leadership positions though they were granted full membership status. Male members were permitted into the OD and women into the Women's Auxiliary. Any prospective citizen could become a school leader, cultural advisor, book attendant, or youth leader. These positions were instrumental in building local group cohesion. They entailed no decision-making authority and were generally nonpromotional. In addition to full members and prospective citizens, the Bund welcomed sympathizers. This group included "those persons who sympathize with our struggle and work and who

The OD (Security Force) as "theatre ushers"

express this sympathy by paying regular donations of money."[16] Denied membership status and privileges, this group's sole contribution was financial. According to membership guidelines, then, anyone willing to subscribe to the principles of the Bund was accepted.

Size of the organization is difficult to establish. Original membership lists and other such documents were destroyed to protect members from slander and personal hardship when the Congressional investigatory committees started their investigations.[17] Given the moribund attraction of Fascist movements, the Bund's size and scope of operation were often exaggerated. Membership figures tended to expand or contract in relation to the emotional climate. Kuhn officially placed membership at 8,299 in a report that the Department of Justice turned over to the Dies Committee in April 1939. The Department found only 6,617 members, of which an estimated 4,529 were concentrated in the metropolitan New York area. However, testifying before the Dies Committee in 1939, Kuhn placed membership at 20,000 with sympathizers three to five times that number. He stated that the Bund was organized in forty-seven states, all but Louisiana. He claimed one hundred local units with fifteen in New York, eight to nine in California, and six in New England. The *New York Times*, in 1937, listed membership at about 10,000. It described the movement as still struggling to amount to something more than just another of the numerous small societies in which Germans like to organize.[18] Testimony given before the New York State Legislative Inquiry in 1938, headed by Senator John McNaboe, indicated ninety-four local organizations functioning nationwide with twenty-two youth-recreational camps and four small weekly newspapers each with circulation found by the

OD (Security Force) opening a rally

Presentation of a youth group

Department of Justice to be about 2,000 copies.[19] A report by the FBI, inserted in the *Congressional Record* by Representative J. Thorkelson of Montana, presented statistics to show the Bund so small that it constituted "no threat," and the Bund's principles of organization were "not destructive to the government of the Untied States."[20] As Americans watched Europe struggle with the meteoric rise of Fascism, they vigilantly monitored all potentially dangerous organizations. Membership figures, real or invented, consequently fluctuated with the temper of the times.

The Bund's structure was enumerated in three documents produced to provide the organizational set-up and administrative and membership regulations.[21] In its own eyes:

> The Bund . . . represents the last possibility of American Germanism to rise from the condition of a down-trodden, war-subjugated disavowed nationality, contented with its lot to the status of a sound, great, proud nationality through which we and our descendents may live according to our own God-given way.[22]

Bundesfuehrer Kuhn presided over the organization, his prescribed goal to:

> Maintain and to extend the German-American Bund as an OFFENSIVE AND DEFENSIVE MOVEMENT OF A NATIONALLY CONSCIOUS GERMAN-AMERICAN PEOPLE, who are national-socialistically and constitutionally dedicated to the service of an actually independent, Aryan-governed United States of America.[23]

The Bund's hierarchy broadened out beneath Kuhn pyramidically. From the top downward were: the

Bundesfuehrer; the national officers, including the Deputy *Fuehrer*, the secretary, the treasurer, a press agent, and a public relations official; officials of the ancillary organizations, including camp directors, the women's and youth auxiliaries, and the DKV (*Deutscher Konsum Verband*, an economic corporation) representative; area regional, city and local *Fuehrers*; and lastly the rank and file membership. The general membership was minutely organized and regimented. The following chart enumerates, in descending order, the "Sovereign Jurisdictions" of the Bund:[24]

> Bund: National
> Areas: Sections (large national areas)
> Regions: Groups of States

Youth night with the Bund in Brooklyn.

Athletic presentation at a Bund meeting

Circuits: Individual States
Districts: Groups of Counties
Precincts: Towns
Squares: Subdivisions of Towns
Blocks: Neighborhoods
House Groups: Subdivisions of Blocks

Each of the subdivisions operated on its own leadership principle, with the local *Fuehrer* responsible for his own area and reporting directly to the *Fuehrer* at the next higher level. Each jurisdiction had specific, precisely defined tasks and responsibilities for each level of authority from the national to the neighborhood level. Lines of communication were such that all members could be informed of events within a twenty-four hour period.[25] By a pre-set means of daily contact with the next higher level of authority, acts of subordinate leaders were always predicated upon approval from the next level up.

In accordance with the leadership principle, communication flowed down from the *Bundesleiter* in a series of Bund Commands. These were issued by Kuhn, as situations necessitated, and were passed down the chain of command. In this manner, Kuhn dictated policy and provided the local commanders, and thus the rank and file membership, with guidelines relevant to the organization.

In addition, card files were maintained at the national headquarters and local offices to keep track of "friends, enemies, merchants, and politicians."[26] White cards were used to identify Bund members and patrons, pink cards for German-speaking nonmembers, green cards for English-speaking nonmembers, yellow cards for enemies, and light blue cards for Jews. Local commanders were to update the card file as necessary.

Annual secret ballot elections were held at each lower level to either maintain or replace that level's leader. Similarly, delegates were sent from each branch to the annual national convention to fulfill the same function on the national level.[27] More often than not, these elections served as votes of confidence, as all officers within the administrative units were appointed by the respective *Fuehrer* of the level above. Under Kuhn's iron hand, this structure resulted in an extremely tight-knit, closely controlled organization relatively free of the dissension that had plagued the Friends.

The primary instrument of Kuhn's control was the Bund's Uniformed Service or OD (*Ordnungs-Dienst*).[28]

Designated by the press as Kuhn's stormtroopers, and by the membership as the Bund's protective arm, the OD was carried over from the Friends and functioned alongside and within the Bund. It was organized at all levels which had the membership and finances to support it. Membership was open to every male Bund member at least eighteen years old, with proof of Aryan origin.

Membership figures for the OD are practically non-existent. It was estimated in a report made by the Committee to Investigate Un-American Activities and Propaganda in 1939 that the German American Bund could muster within its ranks a uniformed force of 5,000 troops.[29] Speaking at the 1938 Bund Convention, Kuhn is recorded as having stated, "I calculate that approximately ten percent of membership should belong to the OD. That is approximately the proportion of the SA to the membership of the NSDAP."[30] Like the general membership figures, statistics concerning the size and power of the OD tended to reflect the degree of concern in the United States. Parallels of the OD and the SA were not overlooked.

The commander-in-chief of the OD was the National Leader of the Bund, in this case Fritz Kuhn. He, in turn, designated a National OD Leader who was charged with the responsibility of maintaining the corps. As would be expected, the OD maintained its own hierarchy and infrastructure. The *Fuehrerprinzip* ruled; absolute obedience was demanded to provide "the assurance that our movement will, at the sacrifice of life if necessary, *remain* the inexorable opponent of Jewish Marxism and the uncompromising champion of the demands of American Germans."[31]

Although weekly musters were used as training sessions for the OD, regulations maintained it was not a

The Uniformed OD (Security Force)

military or even paramilitary body. Training incorporated marching, rifle practice, calisthenics, and singing which was proclaimed to be no more than one
aspect of personal discipline. The Bund publicly
asserted the OD was a group whose major function was
to keep order during meetings and rallies—a role akin
to that of theatre ushers. What the American public
witnessed, however, bore no resemblance to their conception of a theatre usher. Most ominously, the OD was
uniformed—to include Sam Browne belts and armbands.[32] They conducted themselves in strictest military manner and were usually seen en masse—
marching in columns at a parade or demonstration, or
posting the American and Nazi German flags and
retiring to encircle their *Fuehrer* at a rally. That the
Bund publicly dismissed the contention that the OD
was a military unit made no difference—Americans
were convinced that a body of men in the uniform of a
foreign power, marching along American streets, was
a definite threat. Apprehensions were heightened by
the fact that this German-uniformed, jackbooted force
flaunted their Nazism with the Bund salute, identical
to the outstretched arm, open-palmed salute common
in the New Germany. Only for the "Star Spangled
Banner" and "America" was the military salute
required.[33]

Visually, the OD was an impressive force. Apart
from their duties as "theatre ushers," OD men were
quite adept in their primary function which was to
protect the leadership. OD men were undisputably
loyal and ever present. Had they not been, Fritz Kuhn
and other prominent men of his cadre would have
fallen from the many attempts on their lives. Ever
watchful, they were quick to pick up on any act that
had the potential of discrediting the movement. An

aspect of the OD's function is illustrated by a relatively trivial incident which occurred at Camp Nordland, New Jersey. A member of the press, admittedly hostile but freely admitted onto the grounds, had maneuvered a small boy, supplied with a mug of beer, onto a bar. Moving back to snap the boy's picture, the photographer had his camera smashed to the ground and the film destroyed. This action was covered in the press as overt manhandling of the photographer, however, the OD man was commended by August Klapprott, then director of Camp Nordland, for his perception and quick action.[34] The incident indicates the devotion of the OD and the dangers posed by them. It was an obedient force—it could easily be mobilized against any threat.

Oddly enough, arming of the OD was both prohibited by organizational guidelines and practiced in fact. OD

Trooping the line, 1937

men carried no firearms. They were trained in self-defense, however, and generally carried nightsticks and other legal "weapons" which, given their overall presence, made them quite menacing, with or without arms of the technical sense. Generally, within the ranks of the Bund, the OD was considered an elite body. Leadership positions were often filled from the ranks of the OD. Discipline was particularly strict, training was rigorous, and there was much *esprit de corps* within the units. Their position and mission were taken very seriously.[35]

Equally important to the Bund, and threatening to the public, was the formation of youth groups. As in the New Germany, the ideals of the Bund were to be perpetuated through its children. "The youth is our great hope, the life line of our organization," declared the *Bundesfuehrer*.[36] Further:

> Every effort in behalf of the German youth is of great importance over there (Germany), since the future of Germandom in America can no longer depend upon new recruits from across the sea. It must find its German future in its own land, and construct it out of its own youth. Therefore, the youth groups of the German-American Volksbund represent a truly great achievement for Germandom. The children's choirs of the glee clubs help perpetuate the German language. Within the next few years, the entire unified strength of Germandom will be necessary in order to check the shrinkage in the German population through the Americanization of its youth.[37]

With proper education, or indoctrination, the glories of Germanism could be preserved—a feeling of *Deutschtum* instilled. Although political indoctrination was hardly absent, it was this sense of community that prevailed. The children of the Bund pledged their allegiance not only to the Bund's form of National Socialism, and not only to the United States (as incongruous as it may sound), but to their cultural solidarity as well.

Kuhn's youth movement was a carbon copy of Hitler's *Jugend*. Overseen by Youth Division Director Theodore Dinkelacker, the children were divided into two age groups by sex: eight to thirteen and fourteen to eighteen. At eighteen, boys could join the OD or become youth leaders, and girls entered the women's auxiliary. Like other aspects of the Bund, the youth groups were attired in replicas of *Jugend* uniforms complete with swastika buckles and the lightning-bolt insignia which symbolized the power of the Nordic youth to overcome all evil. Children met weekly to participate in a variety of activities that included singing, dancing, arts, crafts, sports, and military drill. During the summer months the children could be sent to one of twenty-four recreational camps owned and operated by the Bund. While the total number of children participating in the movement is not known, in the summer of 1937 nearly two hundred were registered at Camp Hindenburg, near Grafton, Wisconsin, and twice that number were enrolled at Camp Nordland, New Jersey.[38]

Activities in the youth camps were highly regimented. Much time was devoted to the study of *Mein Kampf* and National Socialism in general.[39] A typical day at Camp Nordland began with reveille at six-thirty and ran as follows:[40]

0630	reveille
0640	personal hygiene
0715	tent (or barracks) clean up
0740	tent (or barracks) inspection
0750	roll call

0800	breakfast
0900	work service—chores
1100	swimming
1200	lunch
1300	singing practice
1400	sports
1600	swimming
1800	dinner
1900	singing
1930	group gathering
2100	call to quarters
2130	taps

Representative members of the youth groups were sent annually to Germany to receive instruction and education in National Socialist ideology and technique. One such pilgrimage spent six weeks in the "Fatherland" and participated in a variety of activities to include marching, singing, and attending lectures on National Socialism and anti-Semitism.[41] The leadership felt that these selected youth members could actively span the gulf that separated the Bund from its spiritual homeland, and could, in addition, effectively transmit the glory they had personally witnessed.

Adults as well as the uniformed members of the youth organization had access to the grounds of the recreational camps. The dedication of Camp Nordland, New Jersey, in 1937, indicates its total function:

> Our "camp" is designed principally to be a place which breathes of the spirit of the New Germany. Conscious of this fact, the "camp" is consecrated to our youth. It is there that our boys and girls shall be educated; it is there where the spirit of camraderie and the feeling of belonging to one community is to be inculcated into them; it is there where they shall learn the "you for me and I for you;" it is there where they shall be strengthened and con-

> firmed in National Socialism so that they will
> be conscious of the role which has been
> assigned to them as the future carriers of
> German racial ideals in America.
>   Hereby we give you over "Camp Nord-
> land," to your holy mission. We consecrate
> you as a little piece of German Soil in Amer-
> ica, as a symbol of our motto "obligated to
> America, tied to Germany."[42]

Within the gates of these "little pieces of German soil
in America," former Bundists nostalgically recall
watching athletic demonstrations by the children, and
participating in celebrations and rallies, dances, din-
ing, and camping. The camps were set up to provide the
members with facilities and organized events common
with their cultural heritage. They were cultural havens
for those not yet assimilated; were it not for the swastikas emboldened on the doorways of the buildings, or
the uniformed guards at the gates, the general public
could possibly have allowed the recent immigrants
their homeland away from home. But the Bund presented a stolid and impregnable facade—and the swastikas *were* on proud display.

Fritz Kuhn endeavored to embrace his people with
the Bund. In striving to build a cultural and ideological
society, Kuhn drew the membership into activities that
augmented their lifestyle and beliefs. Bundists
gathered regularly for membership and propaganda
meetings and *Kameradschaft* evenings. They cele-
brated George Washington's birthday, Adolf Hitler's
birthday, Labor Day, German Day, Christmas, and the
celebration of the winter solstice.[43] Within the Bund,
special emphasis was placed on education and the
development of German language and American citizenship schools. Speaker training, music, gymnastics,
and women's services, to name a few, were also offered.

A complete lifestyle could be found within the Bund's social, educational, and cultural activities. Capitalizing on the fact that many recently immigrated German Americans felt socially ostracized in their adopted homeland, the Bund aimed to strengthen the natural ties to the Fatherland and thereby postpone or bypass assimilation. In contradiction, perhaps, the Bund took pains to separate itself from Hitler's NSDAP. To the end, Bundists proclaimed, and believed, themselves to be dedicated American citizens—doing that which, according to their doctrine, would make America stronger and more free. However, their pursuit of Wagnerian Americanism was visibly stamped with the harshness of German National Socialism. Columns of goosestepping, uniformed children and OD men marched against a backdrop of women in *Dirndl* serving beer. However loudly the Bund professed its Americanism, its patriotism was not discernible to the broader American public.

ENDNOTES
Chapter 3

1. *New York Times*, 18 April 1936.

2. Ibid.

3. *Newsweek*, 20 September 1937.

4. Fritz Kuhn, "Awake and Act," 17 April 1936, pp. 1-2. In RG 131, Entry 1, Box 9, National Archives, Suitland, Maryland.

5. The Bund's aims and purposes are listed on page 5 of the tabloid promoting the Pro-American Rally of 20 February 1939, provided to the author by the National Socialist White People's Party.

6. See, for example, Leland V. Bell, *In Hitler's Shadow: The Anatomy of American Nazism* (New York: Kennikat Press, 1973), pp. 19-35; John Carlson, *Under Cover* (New York: E. P. Dutton & Company, 1943), throughout; and Sander A. Diamond, *The Nazi Movement in the United States 1924-41* (Ithaca: Cornell University Press, 1974), pp. 21-31 and throughout.

7. That data was obtained from Fritz Kuhn's "Enemy Alien Questionnaire" which he was required to fill out upon internment. Most of the data cannot be validated due to the age of the documents. Kuhn's transcript of testimony taken by Rhea Whitley, Attorney for the Special Committee on Un-American Activities on 25 March 1939, p. 4, in RG 131, Entry 1, Box 16, National Archives, Suitland, Maryland.

8. John Carlson, *Under Cover*, p. 111.

9. *New York Times*, 30 March 1936.

10. William Seabrook, *These Foreigners* (New York: Harcourt, Brace and Company, 1938), p. 226.

11. Written and oral conversations with former Bundists, taken during the summer and fall of 1982, all of whom request anonymity.

12. For discussions of American Fascism, see Raymond G. Swing, *Forerunners of American Fascism* (Salem, N. H.: Ayer Co. Publishers, Inc., 1935); Richard Pells, *Radical Visions and American Dreams: Culture and Social Thought in the Depression Years* (Middletown, Conn.: Wesleyan University Press, 1977); Lawrence Dennis, *The Coming of American Fascism* (New York: AMS Press, 1977, originally 1936); and Alan Brinkley, *Voices of Protest: Huey Long, Father Coughlin and the Great Depression* (New York: Alfred A. Knopf, 1982) among others.

13. Leland Bell, *In Hitler's Shadow*, pp. 20-21.

14. Sander Diamond, *The Nazi Movement in the United States*, p. 221.

15. Bund Command 3, 30 October 1936. See also Bund Command 18, 3 May 1938. All Bund Commands are found in RG 131, Entry 1, Box 5, National Archives, Suitland, Maryland.

16. Bund Command 18, 3 May 1938.

17. *New York Times*, 17 August 1939.

18. Ibid., 21 March 1937.

19. Ibid., 4 June 1939.

20. Ibid., 21 July 1939.

21. Appendix, Part IV of U. S. Congress, House, Special Committee Hearings on Un-American Activities, 77th Congress, 1st Session, 1941, pp. 1490-1620.

22. Ibid., p. 1582.

23. "Organizational Structure of the Bund," pp. 9-10, found in RG 131, Entry 1, Box 9, National Archives, Suitland, Maryland.

24. Appendix, Part IV, p. 1551.

25. Ibid., pp. 1551-1561.

26. Card file notations found in RG 131, Entry 1, Box 9, National Archives, Suitland, Maryland; also Appendix, Part IV, pp. 1491-1492.

27. Appendix, Part IV, p. 1552.

28. "The OD of the German American Bund," in RG 131, Entry 1, Box 9, National Archives, Suitland, Maryland. See also Department of Justice, *German American Bund*, "Outline of Evidence," September 17, 1942, pp. 24-32.

29. U. S. Congress, House, 76th Congress, 1st Session, *Investigation of Un-American Activities and Propaganda*, January 3, 1939, p. 92.

30. As quoted in Louis DeJong, *The German Fifth Column in the Second World War* (Chicago: University of Chicago Press, 1956), p. 116.

31. Appendix, Part IV, p. 1611.

32. In response to public opinion, the Bund uniform was altered in compliance with Bund Command 6, 26 January 1937, to: black shoes and pants, steel gray shirt, shark gray jacket to have the same cut as that worn by the American National Guard, black ties, armband, black cap and belt with shoulder strap. A further change was made with Bund Command 23, 8 September 1939, in which the uniform was simply black trousers and tie with a gray shirt. The Bund was to be "exemplary in these eventful times."

33. The explanation of the Bund salute is discussed in a flyer promoting the Pro-American Rally of February 20, 1939, provided to the author by the National Socialist White People's Party.

34. Conversation held in August 1982 with former Bundist who requests anonymity.

35. "Rules and Behavior for the OD Man," Appendix, Part IV, pp. 1610-1612.

36. U. S. Congress, House, 76th Congress, 1st Session, Report #2, *Investigation of Un-American Propaganda Activities in the United States* (Washington, D. C.: 1939), p. 98.

37. Excerpt from *Yearbook* (New York: German American *Volksbund*, 1937) in *The German Reich and Americans of German Origin* (New York: Oxford University Press, 1938), p. 41.

38. Additionally, in the summer of 1939, 516 children were registered at Camp Siegfried and 988 at Nordland. See RG 131, Entry 1, Box 2, National Archives, Suitland, Maryland.

39. Department of Justice, *German American Bund*, "Outline of Evidence," September 17, 1942, pp. 33-39.

40. "A Day's Format at *Jung Nordland*," 24 July 1940, in RG 131, Entry 1, Box 2, National Archives, Suitland, Maryland.

41. "Outline of Evidence," pp. 37-38.

42. Excerpt from the pamphlet "Camp Nordland" dated 18 July 1937, in the author's possession.

43. Appendix, Part IV, pp. 1498-1500.

CHAPTER 4

THE
PHOENIX
IN FLIGHT

CHAPTER 4

THE PHOENIX IN FLIGHT

The driving force behind the Bund was the belief that blood was stronger than citizenship or place of birth. Blood and race were the determinants of German mentality, or *Deutschtum*, not environment or location. *Deutschtum*, of course, was that which separated Germans from other peoples. Kuhn appealed to his members on the grounds that Germans were superior to other peoples by virtue of their genetic and cultural heritage, and that racial comrades were linked by a community of blood. This racial elitism was the hallmark of the German American Bund—that which drew the membership and charged the movement with energy.

Racial superiority was a powerful concept to propose to a group of as yet unassimilated people. And it was readily accepted by those who yearned for some sense of identity. Indeed, the call to communion espoused by the Bund was not unlike the cries for white supremacy advocated by the Ku Klux Klan or the fervent fundamentalism of William Pelley's Silver Shirts. All were designed to the same end: to gather together perceptually like-minded people and provide them a haven.

Certainly this concept was not unique to the Bund. Recognizing that Germany's power base was dependent upon its ability to unify the people behind the swastika, Hitler had forged his Third Reich with the dynamic concept of a German Master Race. The unification of all Germans, at home or abroad, was essential to Germany's emergence as a world power. This call to communion was merely echoed by the Bund:

> Present day Germany considers that every person of German ancestry and German blood who adheres to German language and culture is a German racial comrade. Germany does not ask you to neglect your duties as an American, but Germany says, only he who is also a good German can become a good American.

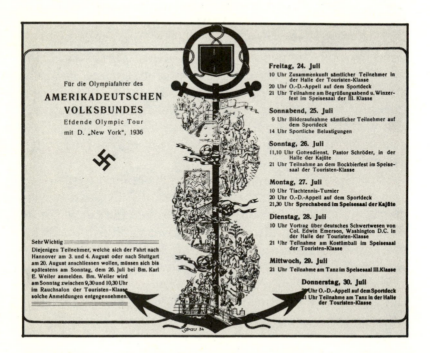

Advertisment for the Bund's trip to Germany

Fritz Kuhn preparing to sail to Germany, 1936

We stand here as the heralds of the Third Reich, as preachers of the German world-viewpoint of National Socialism which has displayed before the eyes of the world the incomparable German miracle, the miracle of National Socialism.[1]

Upon taking control of the Bund in 1936, Kuhn seized this concept of the German master race and used it, much as Germany did, to form an American outpost of National Socialism. Kuhn worked toward the unification of all German Americans under his transplanted swastika.

On board ship to Germany, 1936

The OD (Security Force) shipboard, 1936

This dream drove Fritz Kuhn. And, like his predecessors, he yearned for recognition from Germany. With Germany's resurgence to military and political power, and in conjunction with her status of host of the Olympic Games, Kuhn felt sure that such recognition would be forthcoming.

Obsessed with attaining Hitler's appointment as the American *Fuehrer*, Kuhn and fifty members of the Bund journeyed to the Reich in June 1936.[2] There the group toured such cities as Hamburg, Berlin, Wiesbaden, Stuttgart, and Munich. In Berlin and Wiesbaden, the city mayors and representatives of the VDA welcomed the Bundists. In Stuttgart, the mayor was joined by Fritz Gissibl, former leader of the Friends of New Germany, and other officials of the DAI at a dinner party held in honor of their American guests.[3] Kuhn and his following visited the grave of Horst Wessel, attended Olympic festivals, and marched with the SA through the streets of Berlin. The Bundists were wined and dined and experienced firsthand the ostentation and magnetism of the Third Reich.

Certainly the highlight of the trip was an unexpected audience with Hitler on 3 August. During the short meeting, Kuhn presented Hitler with a leather-bound pictorial history of the Bund, the *Goldene Buch der Amerika-Deutschen*, and a donation of more than two thousand dollars collected by the Bund for the German winter relief program. In the course of the interview, attended also by Dr. Hans Thomsen, Counselor of the German Embassy, Hitler was overheard to tell Kuhn, "Go over there and continue the fight."[4] Kuhn interpreted this comment, and the audience, as indicative of Hitler's interest and intimate knowledge of the Bund. Kuhn was overjoyed at what he perceived to be overt support.

In reality, Hitler's audience with Kuhn seems to be only one of a long procession of meetings by the German head of state with foreign visitors.[5] Germany was, after all, on display, and Hitler played every part the host. Kuhn certainly used the chance encounter to his advantage in hopes of drawing popular support for the Bund. He created quite a furor in the United States and reinforced the belief that Hitler both sanctioned and supported the Bund as an outpost of German National Socialism. Kuhn's trip was given full coverage in the organization's publications and was eagerly picked up by others. Bundists were able to follow every detail of the trip from Kuhn's reception in Berlin, his meeting with Hitler, to the march of a contingent of OD men down the *Unter der Linden Strasse*. A 16 July 1936 issue of the *Voelkischer Beobachter*, the NSDAP's official organ in Germany, declared that *"Bundesleiter*

On board ship to the Fatherland, 1936

Fritz Kuhn is finally creating a permanent movement of German-Americans." In light of the circumstances and times, it was not difficult to come to the conclusion that Germany considered the Bund a viable force in American affairs.

Nevertheless, Kuhn left Germany with no more assurance of support or responsibility than he had come with. He received promises of unlimited supplies of propaganda material but nothing else.[6] His hope to be recognized as the American *Fuehrer* by Hitler never materialized. Kuhn did achieve such status, however, in the eyes of others, as is evidenced by his visit, while in Germany, to the American Ambassador William Dodd. Writing of the meeting in his diary, Dodd described Kuhn as the "Nazi Fuehrer in America" and noted that he believed Kuhn represented the Foreign Office.[7]

Bund on its way to Germany, 1936

Kuhn returned to the United States the American *Fuehrer* in name if not in fact. The fact that he had been in Germany, had participated in Party activities, and had met with Hitler proved a very powerful base from which to operate. From this base Kuhn breathed life and direction into the Bund. Only in historical retrospect does reality, and such details as financial responsibility for the trip, specific meetings and their consequences, matter. In 1936 there was not such discrimination in perspective. Kuhn's trip to Germany and audience with Hitler reinforced the belief, later espoused by Kuhn, that Hitler endorsed the American organization, and that the Party was behind the movement. This perception was of tantamount importance. Without it, it is questionable whether the Bund would have drawn the following it did. Certainly it would not have received the same degree of attention or

Shipboard festivities—to Munich 1936

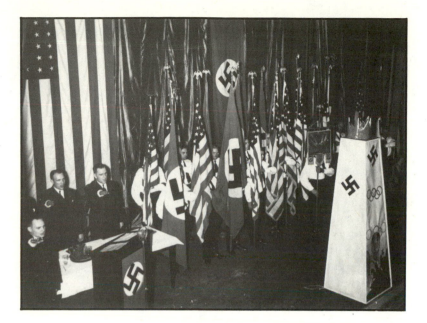

Opening a Bund meeting, 1936
(Fritz Kuhn 3rd from left)

publicity. Indeed, this perception functioned as a double-edged sword. On the one side, Kuhn's personal prestige, influence, and the ability to control and increase membership within the Bund were increased dramatically by the trip. On the other side, however, the perception of Kuhn's links with Hitler and the New Germany would later be used to show proof of un-American activities and conspiratorial ties.

By manipulating the events of the summer of 1936 to enhance his position, Kuhn infused new life into the Bund. Upon returning home he issued Bund Command 1, declaring his allegiance to the cause:

> Today I know better than ever before the direction in which our Bund must go. I know

Christmas Market, DKV (Deutscher Konsum Verband)
German American Business League

that it is not only important to continue our work, I understand that the American-German Bund is called to assume the political leadership of the German element in the United States.[8]

The extent to which the Bund would or could assume political leadership of the mass of German America is debatable. Although Kuhn envisioned a political party built around the Bund, he realized that it would be some time in coming.[9] Certainly at this juncture, enlargement of the membership and consolidation of a power base were considered most essential. Kuhn and his followers had just returned from the New Germany where National Socialism had put on a proud and impressive display. Kuhn naturally brought his impressions home with him, and the idea of transform-

118

ing the "Jew-ridden" United States into a large and magnificent standard bearer of National Socialism was inviting.

Consequently the phoenix took flight. Kuhn began his mission of transplanting National Socialism with the upcoming presidential elections. To Kuhn, the first order of business in making America safe for National Socialism was to unseat President Franklin Roosevelt. To meet that end, the Bund launched a propaganda tirade aimed at Roosevelt, his administration, and his New Deal that rivalled any of Goebbel's efforts in vehemence and hatred. Mobilizing their official newspaper, the *Deutscher Weckruf und Beobachter*, turning out thousands of handbills and pamphlets, and taking every street corner opportunity, the Bund levied scorn and criticism on the administration which had so far been unsuccessful in pulling the United States out of the depth of Depression.[12] Combining anti-Semitism with its bedfellow, anti-communism, the Bund declared that a vote for Roosevelt and his "Jewish dictatorship" would be a vote for the establishment of communism.[11] Blaming all the woes of the world, including the lingering economic Depression and perceived political shift to the Left, on Roosevelt and his administration, the Bund's smear tactics were overwhelming. Such "proof" as FDR's ties to prominent Jewry and his reliance on the Brain Trust (to the Bund, the Jewish Communist clique) was offered to convince those not immediately overwhelmed. The Bund referred to the New Deal as the Jew Deal and warned that the perpetuation of Roosevelt's administration would lead to a complete Communist takeover.[12]

In Bund Command 2, dated 29 October 1936, Kuhn urged his membership, and all of German America in general, to support candidate Alf Landon of Kansas for president.[13] Kuhn's endorsement read:

> I have decided to declare myself in the name of the group for the Republican candidate. We hope from his victory a more friendly position of the United States toward our old Fatherland.[14]

Landon, the Bund claimed, would present a much-needed stand against communism and would favor better commercial relations with Germany.[15] In his unfaltering belief of the solidarity of Germans under National Socialism, Kuhn attempted to draw all German Americans into a solid voting block to defeat Roosevelt. The Bund maintained that the Democratic Party was historically an anti-German party, since it

Fritz Kuhn leading a Bund meeting, 1936

was they who had gotten the United States into World War I and were consequently responsible for the resultant problems which faced their homeland. Some of this "logic" did apparently stir unpleasant memories in the German American community; more German Americans voted for Landon than for Roosevelt.[16] However, the political potential of a unified German America never materialized.

The perception of a politically strong German American bloc remained a definite possibility, however—attractive to the Bund and threatening to many others fearful of growing Nazi power. The Bund had made its mark with the massive propaganda attacks on Roosevelt and his administration. Moreover, the Bund's endorsement of Landon had ramifications on German-

Opening a Bund meeting

Adolf Hitler and Fritz Kuhn, 1936

American relations. The German Embassy in Washington promptly answered the endorsement with a statement of noninvolvement.[17] Furthermore, the Germany Foreign Office in Berlin, in a dispatch to the *New York Times*, categorically denied any involvement in the American electoral campaign.[18] As Germany scrambled to deny Kuhn's intimations of German sponsorship, Kuhn and his followers revelled in the attention. Certainly the opposition that it engendered gave the movement yet another cause to rally around and fight against. The publicity served them well. The years 1936-1938 were years of growth as membership increased and local units expanded to accommodate those drawn to this flamboyant, militant group.

Kuhn used this support to consolidate his organization and place the movement on solid financial ground. Between 1936-1938, Kuhn created or incorporated six independent companies: the German American Business League (*Deutscher Konsum Verband*, or DKV), AV Development Corporation, AV Publishing Company, Prospective Citizens League, German American Settlement League, and the German American Bund Auxiliary.

The most conspicuous of these corporations was the DKV. It had originated with the Friends of New Germany as the German-American Protective Alliance *(Deutsch-Amerikanischer Wirtschafts-Ausschuss*, or DAWA), organized to counter the Jewish boycott against German goods. Although the DAWA collapsed with the Friends, its successor, the DKV, was identical in intent. Its stated purposes were also to counteract the Jewish boycott of German goods and services, and to promote trade between Germany and the United

Hitler acknowledging the Bund, 1936

States.[19] An extremely active agency, the DKV published a yearly trade guide, listed sympathetic firms, offered discounts, sold trading stamps for profit, conducted yearly exhibitions, and participated in New York's Foreign Trade Week.[20] All DKV activities were openly anti-Semitic and naturally pro-Bund. Bundist propaganda and rhetoric were outstanding in all their publications and efforts. The most spectacular event sponsored by the DKV was the 1938 annual Christmas Exposition and Market, held in New York. Advocating "Buy German for Christmas" and "Patronize Gentile Stores Only," the DKV filled the hall with booths of German-made goods.[21] A Ford sedan was given away as the grand drawing prize, and representatives of the German consulate in New York and Bund officials heralded the event as helpful in binding together Germans, Germany and the United States.[22]

Hitler and Goering

Of the other ancillary organizations, the AV Development Corporation administered properties; the AV Publishing Company ran the presses and put out literature; the Prospective Citizens League handled members otherwise unacceptable to membership lists; the German American Settlement League controlled Camp Siegfried, in Yaphank, Long Island; and the German American Bund Auxiliary held the title to Camp Nordland in New Jersey. Tightly administered, these organizations were presided over and controlled by Kuhn in his endeavor to unify his movement and consolidate his power.

He was successful. Bundists, especially in the New York and New Jersey areas where the Bund was most active, found it was possible to live their entire existence within the group's framework. The Bund provided the comradeship that members yearned for and which

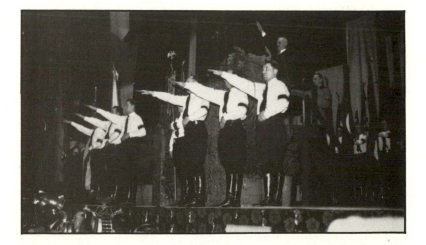

"Sieg Heil"—American style

German Day celebration, 1936

accounted for much of the group's appeal. Cultural heritage was the tie that bound them in an era of economic depression and social change. Social projects were encouraged among the members who rarely left the German American perimeter. The Women's Auxiliary regularly put together bundles of food, clothing, and necessary household utensils for distribution to the needy within the group.[23] Marriages, births, and deaths were handled within the movement, thereby adding to the sense of community. Away from headquarters and the limelight, there was not much of a political cast to the Bund. With the exception of complaints heard in conversation of those gathered for fellowship, a politically oriented radical group was not to be found at the grassroots level of the Bund.[24]

Moving up from this local level, however, the charac-

ter of the Bund changed dramatically. Here the swastikas appeared, ideologically and in substance. At
national and district headquarters levels, National
Socialism was fused to the organization. This is not to
say that the National Socialist bent did not reach to the
base of the membership, for certainly it did, only that it
did not originate there. While the general membership
clung to the Fascist regalia to bring order and stability
to their lives, it was the leadership that was rabidly
National Socialist. Parroting all of Hitler's proposals
for the "betterment of mankind," they intended to
clean up America as Hitler was cleaning up Germany.

Mobilized by Kuhn's powerful invectives, the Bund

German Day festivities

marched as one. Once policy had been set by the *Bundesleiter*, the leadership principle kicked into operation, and the group presented a unified front. Differences in ideology existing between the general membership and the leadership vanished whenever the Bund moved on any particular course of action. Rallied by cries to fight every fight and buoyed by Kuhn's expert administrative skills, the Bund exuded

German Day at Camp Siegfried, 1938

Gathering for fun and festivity, 1938

energetic fervor in its early years. The membership gathered weekly for fellowship, the OD drilled, the presses ran incessantly and spewed out advocation of Aryan power and supremacy, and the recreational camps witnessed continual rallies and celebrations where curiously, the swastikas framed pictures of George Washington.

Because of the Bund's arrogance and bellicosity, the significance of this apparent inconsistency was lost on the general public. The swastikas and jackboots of the movement clouded the group's primal aim—that of the unification of a people and the fortification of a state behind that people. Because the unification of a people would require elimination of the "sub-human" races and fortification of the state implied the domination of National Socialism, any Americanizing aspects of the Bund's doctrine were dismissed as self-serving propaganda. Most Bundists, however, considered America their home and claimed to work only for the betterment of their newly adopted state. It was not difficult, in their minds, to equate their dreams and activities to

those of the Founding Fathers—hence the ever present
posters and references to George Washington. To them,
the Bund was merely beginning the revolution anew.
Instead of fighting against British colonialism, as
Washington and his compatriots had done, the Bund
saw itself as fighting the Jewish-Communist menace
that had insidiously infected America's greatness.
And, technically, within the parameters of a democracy, such thoughts and behaviors are not only
allowed but encouraged. Democracy stands on the
premise that the strength of freedom is more than sufficient to withstand the pulls from the radical fringe
while adopting those principles which are beneficial to
its basic doctrine. To the Bund there was no question as
to their inherent probity. To the FBI, Congress, and
general public, however, the convolutions required in
such thinking were twisted beyond the rational. For

Christmas Market, 1938 DKV (Deutscher Kostum Verband)

the preservation of society and the common good, the organs of democracy launched a crusade to silence this disruptive radical fringe.

The Bund, it seems, had been working at cross-purposes with itself. While their zeal in combatting what they considered "un-Americans"—most notably Jews and Communists—had gained them a notoriety that supplied them with recruits and adherents, it also awakened others to the Fascist challenge.[25] Local concerns throughout the United States began questioning the "Americanism" of the Bund while Congressman Samuel Dickstein of New York, fresh from his successful crusade against the Friends of New Germany, kept pressure on his fellow Congressman to pass a resolution which would authorize an investigation of this new "fifth column."[26]

Although Dickstein's efforts were unsuccessful in

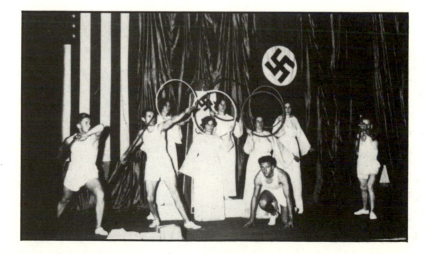

In an Olympic mood—Bund athletic group, 1936

the sense that a Congressional resolution did not materialize, he was extremely adept at influencing the public mood. The rise of anti-Nazi sentiment did not go unnoticed by the Bund. Kuhn, who had taught his followers to welcome every fight, dug in his heels and began a new campaign aimed at convincing the United States of the Bund's loyalty. The German American Bund began the fight for its life.

Kuhn planned to combat Dickstein's deleterious assaults on his organization by deluging Washington with letters extolling the Bund's Americanism. He sent an open letter to Congress which questioned Dickstein's sanity and denied all charges made against the organization as slanderous lies. Similar missives were sent to senators, congressmen, Supreme Court justices, and other federal dignitaries. Local unit leaders were encouraged to do the same on the community level, focusing on state legislators, judges, newspapers,

National Socialism in Los Angeles

Sieg Heil—Free America

"patriotic" club officials, and National Guard officers.[27]

These tactics, employed in all earnestness and sincerity and designed to vindicate the Bund, only served to draw more attention to the organization. In fact, Dickstein could not have asked for a more cooperative target. The Bund, in its naiveté and ignorance of the limits of American tolerance, had led itself to his door.

All this while the phoenix flew as the Bund carried on a dramatic display of spirit and fire. Mass rallies were held in New York City throughout the spring of 1937; notable among them was a rally held at New York City's Hippodrome on 12 February which attracted some 4,000 sympathizers.[28] Heartily denouncing Dickstein and the "Jewish Rabble Rousers" as well as communism, Bolshevism, anti-Fascism, and the anti-Nazi boycott, the Bund hardly mirrored loyal Americanism. In the midst of this zealous activity, anti-Nazi sentiment rapidly increased.[29]

On 18 July, Camp Nordland opened with the ruffles

133

and flourishes of *Deutschland Über Alles* and the
Horst Wessel Lied. As the OD and children's groups
marched under the swastika and Old Glory, August
Klapprott, camp director, and Dr. Salvatore Caridi of
the Union City Italian World War Veterans, led the
opening exercises which were punctuated with cheers
and hails.[30] Members spent the day in festivity and
camaraderie, celebrating the opening of their "little
piece of German soil in America."

Camp Nordland's opening day exercises were a display of the Bund in microcosm. It was proclaimed a
huge success by leadership and members alike, and
denounced as Nazi activity by nearly everyone else.[31]
Nordland, coincidentally located near the New York-
New Jersey water supplies and the Hercules Powder
Plant, came under immediate attack. Commanders of

Herald of the New Germany

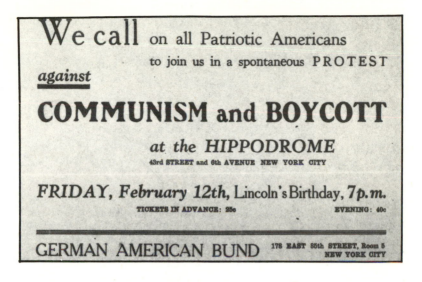

Advertisment for a Bund rally

the New Jersey units of the American Legion and local VFWs called for an immediate investigation of Camp Nordland, dissolution of the Bund, and deportation of its leaders. The Non-Sectarian Anti-Nazi League, a militant organization dedicated to "alerting the public against the menace of National Socialism," sent a host of telegrams to the U. S. Attorney General and numerous congressmen requesting the closing of Bund camps and demanding an investigation of the Bund.[32] This mood was echoed in Congress; Congressmen William M. Citron of Connecticut and Fred A. Hartley of New Jersey petitioned for an FBI inquiry into Bund activities.

Clearly the stage was set and the temper right for Dickstein's proposal to come to life. Dickstein increased his declamations of the Bund, gaining supporters as time passed and tension mounted. His verbal attacks against the Bund were so effective that

135

Why Red Radicals in Public Office by Appointment?

Why Space and Time in the Press and on the Radio for Pinks and Reds, while all Enemies of Jewish-Bolshevism are barred and condemned as

UN-AMERICAN NAZIS AND FASCISTS? !

Why are Patriots losing their Jobs to the "Refugee" Undesirables of Europe?

Why cowardly Mob-Attacks, Riots and Strikes, Ballyhoo Court Cases and Boycotts to cripple all Americans not silent about Red-Jewish

PENETRATION OF AMERICA'S INSTITUTIONS? !

BENJAMIN FRANKLIN'S PROPHECY OF 1789 IS COMING TRUE!

Excerpt from the "JOURNAL OF CHARLES PINCKNEY" of South Carolina of the proceedings of the Constitutional Convention of 1789, regarding the statement of Benjamin Franklin at that convention concerning Jewish Immigration.

"There is a great danger for the United States of America. This great danger is the JEW. Gentlemen, in whichever land the Jews have settled they have depressed the moral level and lowered the degree of commercial honesty. They have created a State within a State and when they are oppressed, they attempt to strangle the nation financially, as in the case of Portugal and Spain.

For more than seventeen hundred years they have lamented their sorrowful fate - namely that they were driven out of their Motherland. But, gentlemen, if the civilized world today should give them back Palestine and their property they would immediately find pressing reasons for not returning there. WHY? Because they are vampires and vampires cannot live on other vampires. They cannot live amongst themselves. They must live among Christians and others who do not belong to their race.

If they are not excluded from the United States by the Constitution, within less than a hundred years they will stream into this country in such numbers that they will rule and destroy us and change our form of government, for which we Americans shed our blood and sacrificed life, property and personal freedom. If the Jews are not excluded, within two hundred years our children will be working in the fields to feed JEWS, while they remain in the counting house, gleefully rubbing their hands.

I warn you, gentlemen, if you do not exclude the JEWS forever, your Children and your Children's children will curse you in your grave. Their ideas are not those of Americans, even when they have lived among us for ten generations. The leopard cannot change his spots. The Jews are a danger to this land and, if they are allowed to enter, they will imperil our Constitution. They should be excluded by the Constitution."

AMERICANS AWAKE! — VOTE FOR F R E E GENTILE CANDIDATES!

Don't stay at home!

Vote for Gentile A N T I - J E W - D E A L Candidates!

VOTE GENTILE!　　　**BUY GENTILE!**　　　**EMPLOY GENTILE!**

Anti-Roosevelt leaflet
136

they prompted Kuhn, in early August, to send a letter to Speaker of the House John H. Bankhead inviting an investigation in an effort to stem adverse publicity and validate his organization and its cause. Kuhn wrote:

> It is with a feeling of profound indignation that I am compelled to submit to the false and malicious statements which Representative Samuel Dickstein is reading in the Congressional Record, and thence supplying to newspapers throughout the country. I have repeatedly asked for an investigation in order to convince the American people that the German American Bund is a patriotic, law-abiding American organization, fighting communism and Marxism as un-American ideals.[33]

A few days later, Kuhn's invitation was accepted. U. S. Attorney General Homer S. Cummings ordered a cursory investigation of German American camps. Maintaining that this action was "more of a check-up than a formal investigation," Attorney General Cummings ordered the FBI to "ascertain if there (were) any facts warranting further investigation."[34] The examination was launched to investigate the allegation that the Bund camps were violating federal laws by shipping unregistered firearms across state lines.

In direct response, Kuhn publicly maintained that he welcomed the investigation, believing it to be the means to stop the harassment and to point out once and for all the loyalty and innocuousness of his movement. "The aim of the German American Bund," declared Kuhn, "is to unite all Germans and Americans in our country to a united front against communism." Ominously he added, "We do show the Nazi emblem alongside of the American flag, with the big-

gest respect for Hitler and his movement in Germany,
fighting the word's madness, communism."[35]

While presenting saint-like bravado to his prosecu-
tors, Kuhn raised the cry of persecution to his membership and the public. Stressing the American ideal of
freedom of speech, Kuhn lashed out with tirades
against Jewish harassment and Communist infiltration. Apparently understanding the dire straits he was
in and the real threat that the investigation posed,
Kuhn gave explicit instructions to his membership
which detailed their expected behavior and which proposed responses:

> The investigation of our entire organiza-
> tion, which has often been a threat and which
> we have repeatedly sought by Congress and
> have openly invited, is now to be introduced
> by the Justice Department. I have explained
> to the Attorney General in a statement about
> our organization (OD, Youth, Women's Auxil-
> iary, Newspaper, DKV, Camps) and about
> our intentions and our objectives and with the
> following, I want to give instructions to the
> Administrators.

> The Local Group Leaders are to advise the
> membership that only he or a member desig-
> nated by him, can give statements to the
> press. Irresponsible conversations with
> strangers are to be discontinued. Many Secret
> Service people are instructed to listen to
> members and assemble information.

> The American German Bund is an Ameri-
> can organization and has no official connec-
> tion with Germany and receives no monies.
> The Bund Fuehrer is not paid by Germany.
> They stand by the statutes and instruct the
> members to read the same.

President Roosevelt is not to be attacked personally in any speech.

Papers of identification are to be asked of persons who represent themselves to be officers, and it must be determined whether such persons have a right to ask questions.

The size and strength of our organization is an official secret, and questions pertaining to this are to be parried. Only before a court or under oath must this question be answered truthfully.

The OD has two great purposes to fulfill:
It serves as a self-protective guard at our meetings and functions against attacks by communists. It preserves order, and serves as a flag guard. It serves all purposes and is called to clear and decorate halls, etc.
The OD is a patriotic group which in the event of necessity will place itself at the disposal of the lawful government. This point is

A Bund group at Camp Nordland

Bund supporters

to be stressed again and again, and the value of the OD is to be explained to the Americans. THE OD IS NOT A MILITARY GROUP. IT IS NOT ARMED.

Our camps first and foremost, are recreational centers for our members. A possibility should be further created so that our youth will have a chance to get off the streets. They are recreational centers for young and old, they serve for sport and play and as an assembly place for people with common views. THEY ARE NOT MILITARY DRILL GROUNDS.

Our newspaper, the *"Deutscher Weckruf und Beobachter"* is the organ of the Bund and naturally has a tendency toward friendliness with Germany.

The D.K.V. is an economic organization of our Bund and its objective is to establish a

4 / *The Phoenix in Flight*

society of interest between the business people and the consumers. It is a self-defensive organization against the unconstitutional boycott of German goods.

In brief: We are an American organization, and all that we do is done within the law and for the welfare of the United States. We have no official connection with Germany and we receive no orders from there and are not paid from there. WE DO NOT THINK OF OVER-THROWING THE GOVERNMENT.

We desire that the constitution of the country be upheld. We permit no agitation and lies against Germany, and we fight without compromise every Marxist thought, and above all else we are opposed to communism and its Jewish leaders. We want to acquire influence in the law formulating processes of this country for the German people, but according to the law. BEYOND THIS ONLY THE LOCAL GROUP LEADER GIVES OFFICIAL DECLARATIONS.[36]

Kuhn's admonitions to the membership, directing them to be cautious in their public presentations, were hardly enough to stem the rising tide of public intolerance. Nor was his directive even complete within itself. The image of the Bund was polished, but the threat which the image represented was not diminished by the attempted alterations. Although Kuhn had given detailed directions to his membership concerning "correct" information to be given out, nothing was done to tone down the general appearance of the organization or its propaganda stance. Still the presses rolled out their standard line which condemned Jewish persecution and exalted Aryan greatness; still the uniforms were flaunted and rallies held. In fact, little more than a month after issuing Bund Command 13, Kuhn organized the "Citizens' Monster Rally" in New York City.[37] Exhibiting the strength of his movement, Kuhn charged his audience to awake and assume the greatness inherent in National Socialism.

In effect, then, the stance of the Bund remained unchanged. Not, however, public opinion. As the Bund continued to march, adverse public opinion grew steadily. Unaware, or unaffected, by Kuhn's meager attempt to cloak his movement in Americanism, outcries from local and community levels only sparked further apprehension and suspicion. In November, Judge J. Wallace Leyden, in Bergen County Naturalization Court in New Jersey, echoed America's fears as he warned applicants he would deny them citizenship with proof of Bund membership. Winning high praise from the local press, law enforcement officials and Samuel Dickstein anxiously waiting in the wings, Judge Leyden proclaimed, "You can't be both an American and a German. You must be either one or the other. I consider membership in the German American Bund sufficient grounds for denying citizenship. (It is) obvious that a person believing in dictatorships cannot also believe in the American form of government."[38]

This was the wellspring from which the House Un-American Activities Committee emerged. Despite the fact that, on 5 January 1938, Attorney General Cummings released his report on the FBI investigation of the Bund which cleared the organization of any federal wrongdoing, America mobilized a campaign designed to cleanse herself of any and all foreign infiltration. The German American Bund, vehemently vocal and militarily garbed, was an obvious target.

ENDNOTES
Chapter 4

1. *Yearbook*, New York, German American Volksbund, 1937, from RG 131, Entry 1, Box 10, National Archives, Suitland, Maryland. Also *The German Reich and Americans of German Origin* (New York: Oxford University Press, 1938), p. 42.

2. Although travel arrangements were made by a German travel agency, each individual paid his own trip expenses. Local Bund units raised money through collections, and a Benefit Ball was held at the Yorkville Casino in New York on 13 June 1936 which raised $3015 for the trip. See *Deutscher Weckruf und Beobachter*, 18 June 1936.

3. *Deutscher Weckruf und Beobachter*, 10 September and 1 October 1936.

4. As recorded by George Froeboese, head of the Midwestern Department of the Bund, in the Bund's *Yearbook*, New York, 1937, pp. 55-56.

5. *New York Times*, 16 October 1936. Dr. Thomsen indicates that the meeting was routine.

6. Propaganda was supplied, throughout the life of the organization, by the VDA. See Donald M. Mckale, *The Swastika Outside Germany* (Ohio: The Kent State University Press, 1977), pp. 55-58.

7. Martha and William E. Dodd, *Ambassador Dodd's Diary* 1933-38 (New York: Harcourt, Brace and company, 1941), I: 340.

8. Bund Command 1, 28 October 1936. All Bund Commands are found in RG 131, Entry 1, Box 5, National Archives, Suitland, Maryland.

9. Taken from a taped conversation with a former Bundist, who requests anonymity, August 1982.

10. It is important to note that the German American Bund was not alone in its dissatisfaction with the Roosevelt regime. A myriad of groups voiced their displeasure as well. For a sampling, see John Carlson, *Under Cover* (New York: E. P. Dutton and Company, 1943); and Alan Brinkley, *Voices of Protest: Huey Long, Father Coughlin, and the Great Depression* (New York: Random House, 1983).

11. *New York Times*, 16 October 1936.

12. *Deutscher Weckruf und Beobachter*, September and October 1936.

13. Bund Command 2, 29 October 1936.

14. *New York Times*, 16 October 1936.

15. Ibid.

16. Louis L. Gerson, *The Hyphenate in Recent American Politics and Diplomacy* (Lawrence: University of Kansas Press, 1964), pp. 33, 119-120. See also Samuel Lubell, *The Future of American Politics* (New York: Harper and Row, 1965) p. 133. Howard Allen found that in counties where citizens of German stock were in the majority, balloting turned strongly against Roosevelt. See Howard W. Allen, "Studies of Political Loyalties of Two Nationality Groups," *Journal of the Illinois State Historical Society* 57(1964): 146.

17. *New York Times*, 16 October 1936.

18. Ibid., 18 October 1936.

19. Letter from Willy Luedtke, DKV National Leader, to the Board of Trade for German American Commerce, Inc., 7 August 1937, RG 131, Entry 6, Box 1, National Archives, Suitland, Maryland. See also U. S. Department of Justice, *German American Bund*, "Outline of Evidence," pp. 39-40.

20. Memos and papers on the DKV found in RG 131, Entry 6, Box 2, National Archives, Suitland, Maryland.

21. "Outline of Evidence," p. 40.

22. Leland V. Bell, *In Hitler's Shadow: The Anatomy of American Nazism* (New York: Kennikat Press, 1973), p. 32. Papers on the Christmas Exhibition found in RG 131, Entry 6, Box 1, National Archives, Suitland, Maryland.

23. Material gathered on the social aspects of the Bund in taped interviews with numerous female former Bundists, August 1982.

24. Information solicited from a questionnaire developed by the author and circulated to surviving Bundists by the current National Socialist White People's Party, summer 1982.

25. The Bund alone was not responsible for this, however. There were at least dozens of organizations parroting some form of Fascism, some quietly, some not. As disturbing as the threat of encroaching Nazism was, it was made more so by the number and diversity of Fascist groups sprinkled throughout the United States. Most groups were not associated in anything even akin to a united front, as the HUAC would later attempt to prove, choosing to retain their autonomy while jealously guarding their perceived exclusiveness. For instance, Lawrence Dennis, the influential intellectual exponent of National Socialism, had very little to do with the German American Bund, characterizing them as rabble rousers. See John Carlson, *Under Cover*, pp. 463, 481-500.

26. Dickstein unsuccessfully introduced a resolution to Congress in January 1937 which would have authorized the formation of an investigatory committee.

27. Leland Bell, *In Hitler's Shadow*, pp. 55-56.

28. *New York Times*, 13 February 1937.

29. Indicative of the public mood was the support given to Mayor LaGuardia's (New York) suggestion that a bust of Hitler be made the central figure of a Chamber of Horrors at the New York World's Fair. Some 83% of the letters received following his remark conveyed approval. See *New York Times*, 9 March 1937. Major Julius Hochfelder, attorney for the German-American League for Culture (an anti-Nazi organization formed in October 1935 in opposition to the

Friends of New Germany) requested a conference of anti-Nazi organizations to gather evidence against Kuhn. See *New York Times*, 23 March and 2 April 1937.

30. Martha Glaser, "The German American Bund in New Jersey," *New Jersey History* 92/1 (1974): 40.

31. For a chronicle of anti-Nazi activity following the opening of Camp Nordland, see Martha Glaser, "The German American Bund in New Jersey," pp. 40-41.

32. Leland Bell, *In Hitler's Shadow*, p. 56.

33. *New York Times*, 11 August 1937.

34. Ibid., 19 August 1937. The FBI had been alerted, and set in action, by Roosevelt, as early as 25 August 1936. Primarily concerned with the activities of Constantine Oumansky, Counselor for the Soviet Embassy in Washington, a direct appeal was made to Hoover to investigate all infiltrative groups and activities. See Don Whitehead, *The FBI Story* (New York: Random House, 1956), pp. 157-162.

35. *New York Times*, 19 August 1937.

36. Bund Command 13, 14 September 1937.

37. The "Citizens' Monster Rally" was held in New York City's Hippodrome on 30 October 1937. See *New York Times*, 30 October 1937.

38. *New York Times*, 20 November 1937.

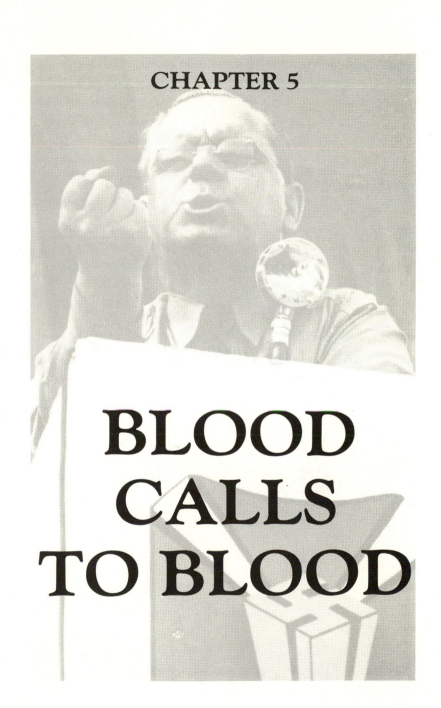

CHAPTER 5

BLOOD
CALLS
TO BLOOD

CHAPTER 5

BLOOD CALLS
TO BLOOD

Attorney General Cummings' pronouncement of innocence of the German American Bund opened the floodgates for *Bundesleiter* Kuhn. Cleared of any federal wrongdoing by the FBI, Bund headquarters rocked with jubilation. Kuhn's perception of the democratic process was such that he interpreted the Attorney General's statement as definitive—a final closing of the books on any attempt to dislodge the Bund. Believing that to be democracy's go-ahead signal, Kuhn's phoenix soared higher. The Bund saw itself as without credible enemies and moved to fulfill its ambition of taking what it saw as its rightful place in America. Recruitment drives were initiated and moves were made to increase the circulation of the group's publication, the *Deutscher Weckruf und Beobachter*. Gerhard Wilhelm Kunze, the Bund's publicity director and Deputy *Fuehrer*, was sent on a speaking tour throughout the east and midwest with the authority to create new units.[1] Celebrating their victory on 30 January 1938, the Bund held a mass rally at New York City's Turnhalle in honor of the anniversary of the founding of the Third Reich.[2]

Although the FBI could find no evidence to indict the Bund, the general American public had no trouble doing so. As Bundist activity increased, so did anti-Nazi activity.[3] Whether or not the investigative agencies in Washington could find evidence of subversion or infiltration, citizens at home who witnessed the Bund's activities, read of their exploits, and heard their claims found definitive parallels between the German American Bund and National Socialist Germany and were not content to let the threat go unanswered. For example, a Bergen County, New Jersey, meeting of the Bund, held at a private residence, ended in fisticuffs prompted by members of the American Legion in opposition to the Bund.[4] Labor organizations in Reading, Pennsylvania, declared their intention to resist any attempt by the Bund to establish a recreational camp in their area.[5] A series of fist fights broke up a meeting of nearly seven hundred in Buffalo, New York, as Gerhard Kunze attempted a membership drive.[6] Labor organizations, veterans' groups, and "patriotic" clubs took to the streets, often with accompanying violence, to demonstrate against Bund infiltration and the dictatorship in Germany.

This activity, by no means limited in its direction against the German American Bund, was part and parcel of a general fear that swept the United States prior to World War II.[7] Concerned primarily with Communist doctrine and the aggressive stance of the Comintern, whose expressed aim was to stimulate worldwide revolution, it embraced the fear of the growing militant dictatorships in Europe which sought world domination. America, relatively complacent in her physical security, began to anticipate infiltration by fifth columns.[8]

The fear of fifth column invasion was spawned by groups based abroad, such as the Comintern in the Soviet Union and Hitler's NSDAP, and perpetuated by agencies either based in or transmitting to the United States. As such, the reaction was not without foundation. And, once the perception of fifth column infiltration took hold, reinforced in large part by groups such as the German American Bund, it validated itself. However, in order to accurately assess the general fear directed at the Third Reich in historical retrospect, it is imperative to review the foundation and the resultant perceptions it engendered.

In 1936, seventy-four official and unofficial agencies existed in Germany that were concerned with Germans living beyond the borders.[9] Most of them carried out routine functions such as the handling of exchange students, religious conferences, tourist services, and information distribution. By far, most were innocuous in intent and discreet in practice. Some, however, were

A Bund meeting

Fritz Kuhn

not so benign. As Nazification intensified in the New
Germany, agencies that had espoused pan-Germanism
and cultural unity previously were easily brought
under Party domination and became transmission
belts for National Socialist propaganda.

Of the more aggressive agencies which dealt with
Germany's citizens abroad, mention has already been
made of the AO, APA, DAI, and VDA and of their
relationship with the Friends of New Germany.

Although Germany disavowed the Friends in 1935, potential relationships between American-German groups and the Reich were still possible and the cry for the unification of all Aryans under the swastika continued. Once the House Committee began to investigate the Friends and discovered those links, they were to remain forever suspect.

Given the fact that Goebbel's Propaganda Ministry had jurisdiction over all German organizations at home and abroad, at least the suspicion of active Party support of these organizations was perceptually correct. Ominously, the most dominant of the agencies under Goebbel's supervision, the Foreign Section of the NSDAP, or AO, was placed under Rudolf Hess after October 1933, thus elevating it in the sphere of Party control and prestige. It would be this particular link that later came to indicate German sponsorship. Equally threatening to the American public were Hitler's cries for the establishment of a world-wide racial community and the practice of dual nationality. Initiated in 1913, this bureaucratic procedure enabled German citizens to retain their German citizenship while accepting that of another country. Thus, proof of American citizenship was not necessarily indicative of renunciation of German allegiance.

By far, however, the perceived link between Germany and German American groups espousing National Socialism was forged through propaganda dissemination. Indeed, the Third Reich was built on the belief of a blood communion and the unification of all Germans, and propaganda to this effect was widespread. Its mass and timber was not only overwhelming, but also glaringly apparent to the press which dutifully passed on the information to their public. The Bund embraced these doctrines and heartily supported them. The implication of German sponsorship was a logical conclusion. In retrospect, it appears much more innocuous. For instance, when Kuhn received assurance of unlimited propaganda materials in 1936, his organization was merely added to the mailing lists of various organizations designed to disseminate National Socialist ideology. Given the temper of the times, however, it was the perception, rather than the reality, which carried.

Beyond the AO, DAI, VDA, the German Foreign Ministry, and the Foreign Affairs Office of the NSDAP, agencies that engaged in propaganda dissemination included the Transocean News Service, the German Library of Information, and the German Railroads Information Office. These agencies developed National Socialist propaganda which was transmitted in bulk to a host of Nazi front groups, isolationist organizations, the consulates, and private citizens working for the German cause.[12]

The Transocean News Service was a press organization designed by the German Foreign Office, operated by the Propaganda Ministry, and directed in the United States by Dr. Manfred Zapp.[11] It was devoted to news propagation, strictly towing the Party line, and the dissemination of propaganda, much of which was collected by the German Embassy consulates in the United States. Included on its mailing lists were German language newspapers, private citizens, and the German consulates in Chicago, San Francisco, St. Louis, Cleveland, Mobile, Boston, New York City, Washington, D. C., and New Orleans.

The German Library of Information, headquartered in New York City, was created in May 1936 by the Reich to disseminate pertinent information concerning art, literature, and scientific and cultural achievements of Germany. It was organized by the Propaganda Ministry and operated under the direction of the Consulate General in New York. Its most influential publication, the weekly *Facts in Review*, was found to have a circulation of between 75,000 and 220,000, supplied to libraries, radio stations, newspapers, and prestigious American citizens.[12]

The German Railroads Information Office, also headquartered in New York City, was under the jurisdiction of both the Propaganda Ministry and the German Foreign Ministry. It worked primarily with travel bureaus, sending out advertising material which portrayed the benefits of travel in Germany. It also sent out a weekly newsletter, *News Flashed from Germany*, with a circulation of approximately 125,000. Basically it was subtle propaganda which concentrated on pictorial accounts of the good life in the Fatherland.

These agencies, set up and maintained by the German government, were propaganda outposts. Even though they funneled money and material, a fifty-year-old Trojan Horse does not appear to be a threat. However, at the time there was much concern over the volume of German propaganda reaching the American public.[13] To many in the United States, it signalled a National Socialist conspiracy which threatened the American way of life. The stresses undergone by a nation moving towards war produce spies and conspirators, both real and imagined, behind every door.

For his part, Kuhn continued to make much of his ties and communications, valid or otherwise, with the Third Reich. Indeed, as *Bundesfuehrer* of the American outpost of National Socialism, those ties were his claim to legitimacy and personal fame. The extent to which claims of German benefaction were justified is a moot question when the situation is viewed contemporaneously. That Kuhn's braggadocio disturbed the United States is a foregone conclusion. Unbeknownst to Kuhn, however, his organization and its bellicose stance worried the Reich as well.

History had not gone unnoticed by Hitler. He was acutely aware of the need to keep the United States out of Germany's sphere of influence.[14] His mobilization for expansion within Europe, and the foreign policy developed for its execution, was implemented with the world community in mind. All territorial demands were made domestically, with the stress upon incorporating like peoples and territories. England and France's appeasement efforts indicated not only their deep desire to avoid a second world war, but also a basic agreement with the logic of Hitler's claims. If the United States could be similarly appeased by the persuasiveness of German doctrine and influenced by the political naivete of her Allies, Hitler would be assured of the European continent.

Hitler had, of course, managed to alienate the majority of Europe and thus left himself isolated. That seems to have been a necessary result when one considers the tenets of National Socialism. The development and strengthening of the Master Race could not be made possible without it. In order to establish one's people as superior, negative comparison is unequalled. It is most obvious in Hitler's treatment of the Jews and Slavs— the so-called "subhumans." With the political development of the New Germany came propaganda to the effect that the United States was dominated by Jews. German propaganda took full advantage of this and peppered its press, both at home and abroad, with denunciations of America along those lines. Here was a dichotomy of Germany policy. On the one hand, it sought to soft-pedal relations with the United States in

Bund rally

order to keep her away from thoughts of European intervention. At the same time, it had to bring to the fore the negative comparisons and derogatory stance demanded by National Socialism. Faced with this dilemma, Hitler chose first the establishment of a solid National Socialist Germany, thinking that unfavorable publicity could be undone and smoothed over when the time came.[15] Therefore, until 1936, the United States was both dealt with cordially and held in much disdain.

The years immediately preceding the war show a change in German tactics in its treatment of the United States. The Reich's reticence in its press relations dealing with the United States shows uncommon restraint. This policy was aimed at creating a sense of security within the United States to avoid provision of any cause for agitation by interventionists. After 1936, Germany's aim was to counter discontent that the

157

German American Bund and internal events in Germany had aroused in the United States.

Towards this end, Hans Luther was replaced as German Ambassador in the United States by Hans Dieckhoff in May 1937. A career diplomat, Dieckhoff had become head of the Anglo-Saxon section of the Foreign Ministry in 1930, and had considerable experience with both the United States and Great Britain. German American movements were not unfamiliar to him. In March 1934, he had communicated to the German Embassy in the United States that inasmuch as the continued boycott as well as the agitation by the press were worsening the feeling against Germany, he thought it "urgently desirable" to prevent additional fuel from being added to the fire as a result of investigations by a Congressional Committee.[16] His comments

A Bund meeting

referred to the on-going examination of the Friends by the Dickstein-McNaboe Committee.

By the time Dieckhoff assumed the reins at the consulate, the German American Bund had consolidated and certainly made an impact. Thanks, in part, to a speech Kuhn had made in August 1937, where he insinuated he had a "special arrangement" with Adolf Hitler, increased numbers of Foreign Ministry and Party officials realized that the Bund actively stimulated the deterioration of diplomatic relations between the two nations.[17] While its activities were in no way being monitored by the German Embassy, the Bund had begun to be a major topic of conversation. In October 1937, the American Charge d'Affaires in Berlin, Prentiss B. Gilbert, paid a visit to the Foreign Ministry at the behest of the State Department to express concern over the effects of the conduct of Germans in the United States on German-American relations. He noted the belief that "these German colonies" took their orders from Germany. He recommended that the AO be informed that unease was only increased by "parading of Germans in brown uniforms and [by] anti-democratic statements."[18] Gilbert's recommendation was followed up by the Foreign Office, and the conclusion of the AO was that to better relations between Germany and America it would be advisable to cut relations with the Bund. Senior Counselor Hans Freytag asserted in a memo dated 11 October 1937 that the NSDAP had nothing to do with German American clubs; there was no connection whatsoever between the German government and the German American Bund.[19] He went on to advocate the demise of the Bund but suggested its collapse would not be in Germany's best interest unless it could be replaced by another organization built along cultural lines.

Upon assumption of his ambassadorial post, Dieckhoff had the opportunity to observe the Bund and monitor the reactions it produced in its homeland. In a
dispatch dated November 1937, he pointed out that the
activities of the German American Bund were suspected of being directed from Germany, and that the
suspicions resulted in odious comparisons being
drawn between the Comintern and a similar "Nazintern."[20] Dieckhoff worried that the Bund would unwit-
tingly sabotage his efforts to prevent a break in diplomatic relations between the two countries. He
complained that, "Nothing has resulted in so much
hostility toward us in the last few months as the stupid
and noisy activities of a handful of German-Americans."[21]

Statements given as well by the German Consul
Generals of New York and Chicago indicated that the
manner of the Bund leaders had led to the ever-
increasing resistance and resentment of American
public opinion and of official agencies.[22] Their statements agreed that German-American relations were
aggravated by boastful remarks in public by inexpe-
rienced Bund leaders concerning alleged secret relations with the government and Party authorities in
Germany. Additionally, they noted that public opinion
maintained the Bund could not function without at
least the moral support of the German Party
authorities.

On 7 January 1938, Dieckhoff submitted an inten-
sive and detailed study of the history of the German
element in the United States and the effect of this
history on the current relations between the German
American Bund and the United States.[23] His initial
finding was that the German American element in the
United States was basically useless, mainly because of

its size. Although there were at most twelve to fifteen million German Americans in America, he postulated no more than one third of them could read or speak German or be expected to have any feeling of *Deutschtum*. He felt that the possibility that this small segment could become a dynamic foundation for National Socialism in the United States was remote. He maintained that political unity under Fascism was virtually impossible among such diverse splinters. In the Chicago area, Dieckhoff found, of the approximately 700,000 German Americans, only 40,000 belonged to some German-oriented club, and only 450 were members of the Bund.[24]

While he extolled the aims of the Bund, Dieckhoff initially denigrated its methods. He asserted that it had failed to key its campaign to the American mentality and thus had isolated itself. Such trappings as the uniforms and usage of the German flag had convinced even pro-German Americans that the Bund was a German rather than an American organization. That Bund leaders claimed to have instructions from Party authorities did not help Germany's propaganda stance. Therefore Dieckhoff proposed a policy to divorce the Foreign Ministry from the Bund. He advocated:[25]

1. Germany should pursue no aims among the German element in America,
2. Political contact between Germany and the Bund must be stopped,
3. Adherence must be demanded to the decision that Reich Germans must withdraw from the Bund,
4. Reich authorities must not concern themselves with the internal affairs of the Bund, and,

> 5. An open disavowal of the Bund by the German government should be considered only as a last resort.

In spite of his sharp criticism, Dieckhoff believed the Bund could still be of service to the Fatherland. Like Freytag, he curiously advised against an irreparable, open break with the Bund.

In response to Dieckhoff's dispatch, meetings of the Cultural-Political Section of the Foreign Ministry were held throughout January and February 1938.[26] Present were representatives from the VDM, the AO, the Ministry of Propaganda, and political and intelligence divisions of the Foreign Ministry. It was agreed that Kuhn should be told that Germany would no longer tolerate the presence of its nationals in his organization, and the group was forbidden the use of Party insignia. It was determined that should Kuhn venture a trip to Germany he would be received by a representative of the VDM only, the agency delegated to monitor ethnic Germans abroad, and would be forbidden to discuss the Bund publicly while in Germany.[27]

The Foreign Office thus recommended the end of the questionable liaison between the Party and the Bund. German consuls were instructed to exhaust every possible means to expedite the above directives. Moreover, Dieckhoff was instructed to call on Secretary of State Hull to inform him of the decision, which he did on the 28th of February.[28] Measures were thereby taken to prove to the United States Germany's basic noninterference. Ostensibly it was maintained that Germany could not allow the development of any German element that would endanger German-American relations, but it was hoped that cultural activities could be maintained.

Germany's willingness to reject the Bund produced mixed reactions. Generally, U. S. State Department officials reacted favorably to the move in policy.[29] Charge d'Affaires Gilbert was convinced that the German government would not encourage in any way "any organization affecting the domestic political affairs of the United States."[30] Secretary of State Hull was also impressed by the adroit diplomacy.[31] On the other hand, the *New York Times* and news magazines such as *Time* reported that Dieckhoff's statement was only a reiteration of the October edict of 1935 which had ordered all German nationals out of the Friends of New Germany.[32] Considering the outcome of the 1935 edict, they could see no reason to take Germany at her word.

Mixed reaction or no, the Reich government had publicly disavowed the Bund. Certainly it had been an essential political move—Germany had to make the effort. In February 1938, when the March of Time had asked the German consulate to preview its film on the National Socialist movement in Germany and the United States, the official German pronouncement was that of objection directed against the inclusion of scenes of Kuhn's meetings and the Bund's summer camps.[33] Kuhn was proclaimed a nuisance.

The Bund's response to the change in policy was, "We take orders from no one, German or otherwise."[34] Bund leaders publicly affirmed that they would devote themselves to "American Nazism" based on the proposal to "rescue America from communism and Jews."[35] Despite this independent stance, Kuhn had been stung by the Foreign Office's repudiation of the Bund. Realizing its implications for the future of the movement, Kuhn decided to visit the Fatherland to convince the Foreign Ministry that the Bund was a

A Bund meeting

valuable asset rather than a costly liability. He realized that the Bund needed at least tacit support from the Reich to survive.

Kuhn arrived in Belgium on the first of March to attend an anti-Communist conference called in Brussels by the Belgian Fascist leader Leon Degrelle.[36] From there he proceeded to Germany. This time there were no parades, social functions, and no audience with Hitler. Kuhn's contact was limited to Hitler's aide, Captain Fritz Wiedemann. During the meeting Kuhn argued for support of his organization and defended its policies and procedures. Despite Kuhn's insistence that the organization furthered German interests, Wiedemann only reinforced decisions made earlier. Several points were brought out by Wiedemann in his response to Kuhn that deserve attention. When queried as to the value placed on the Bund by the Foreign Ministry, Wiedemann's response was:[37]

1. You are an American citizen; I have, therefore, no instructions to give you . . .
2. You are not acting honestly insofar as you
   make unfair use of previous conversations
   with Reich-German officials . . .
3. I shall not discuss with you anything that
   is beyond the duties of the *Volksdeutsche
   Mittelstelle*.
4. The termination of membership in the
   German-American Bund by Reich-
   Germans is a final decision.
5. The German-American Bund has made relations between the German and American
   governments more difficult, . . . it . . . was
   bound to arouse the distrust of the American government.

Kuhn was, to say the least, unsuccessful in his efforts
to persuade the authorities of the Bund's potential.
This time, in leaving Germany, he left not only with
something less than recognition, but with something
less than respect.

Passage back to the United States was long indeed.
For a man who had devoted his livelihood to the support, maintenance, and growth of this semi-political,
wholly fraternal group; fate, in the guise of the German
government, had played a cruel trick. Kuhn was no
doubt perplexed. Why the rejection? The Bund was
modelled after the New Germany, and modelled well.
Even Dieckhoff had commented favorable on its
organization. In his words, the Bund was praiseworthy
as it "unite(d) aggressive young German-Americans,
carrie(d) on the fight against Jews and Communists,
and advocate(d) an American racial policy."[38]

Kuhn had succeeded in bringing Hitler's Germany to
the United States. His *Amerikadeutscher Volksbund*
was spread throughout the United States, although in
admittedly small, almost isolated cells. Within these

cells, loyalty and satisfaction provided the cement that fed the group despite growing suspicion of the press and public. For this, Kuhn assumed his efforts would be recognized and lauded. However, in his zealous efforts to construct and sustain this Germanic enclave, Kuhn failed to note the changing times. Driven by his intense hope of German recognition, Kuhn had constructed a viable radical group in America's heartland. Buoyed by the brace of America's version of personal liberties and freedoms, Kuhn failed to heed the balance maintained between those freedoms and the country's needs.

For the moment, however, Kuhn was faced with a choice. He had rushed to Germany to make a personal appeal, to plead his case. He lost. He could return to his people and announce the defeat as would have been in keeping with the leadership principle. Were Kuhn the Hitler loyalist or stooge he has been portrayed to be, that is what he would have done. As successful as he had been in reorganizing and revitalizing the Bund, it would be naive to believe that Kuhn did not realize his potential. Certainly it would have been relatively easy for him to abandon his American effort to pursue what could have been a promising career in Germany.

Kuhn's second choice was to disregard Germany's instructions and continue "the fight" regardless of support. That is what he did. While purposely not so well publicized as his first trip to Germany, Kuhn's venture to the Reich and the announcements from the consuls demanding withdrawal from the Bund of all Reich-Germans were well known. Kuhn had only to mislead his followers about the "success" of his recent trip to perpetuate his perceived position. He was, after all, adept at exaggeration and half-truth. Indeed, his homecoming boast was that he had been in contact with Goering and Goebbels and had received instructions from them and *Volksdeutsche Mittelstelle*.[39] Ambassador Dieckhoff was so amazed by these assertions and of others that claimed friendship with the German elite that he initiated an investigation. The Ministry reported back that "the natural conclusion is that Herr Kuhn was—as on other occasions—consciously deviating from the truth in order to strengthen his position with his adherents."[40]

Undaunted, on 3 May 1938, following his return to New York, Kuhn issued Bund Command 18, calling for the reorganization of the movement:

> I returned from Europe a few days ago strengthened by the great experience of the reunion of Austria with the Fatherland, and by the conscientious work which has made our homeland stronger, more beautiful, peaceful and larger. My observations of the work of the growing anti-communistic movements in other lands have taught me that we too are on the right path. Our fight too is going successfully forward. The increasing, sharp persecutions to which we are exposed, and to which we will be increasingly exposed, prove clearly that the opponents respect and fear us.
>
> Various changes are imminent, but they are not changes which affect the fundamental principles of the movement. All hindering movements must be done away with, and a clear direction must be laid down from which no deviation must be permitted. The internal organization of our movement must be sharpened.[41]

Kuhn's plan of action was to Americanize the Bund. In dealing with Germany's *diktat*, Kuhn urged all nationals to take out first papers towards American citizenship—this applied to members of the Prospective Citizens League as well.[42] In response to the ban on the use of Party insignia, several slight modifications were made. From this time on, the Bund would no longer fly the German Reich flag except at special demonstrations and then only in conjunction with the American flag. As a result of the edict, a Bund flag was developed to replace that of the New Germany. The background of this new flag consisted of black, white, and red rays in the pattern of a Maltese Cross upon which the emblem of the Bund, a swastika on the base of an inverted pyramid, rested.[43] Thus, the bund did move to adopt a separate style. The differences were minor, however, and undetectable to on-lookers. The Bund had made its mark—the impression left by one pair of jackboots could not be altered.

Moving to increase membership and broaden the movement's appeal, an English section was added to the *Deutscher Weckruf und Beobachter*. Lauded as further proof of Americanization, the insert, the *Free American*, comprised a few pages of an otherwise totally Germanic publication. Its inclusion was an admission of waning support.

The changes instituted by Kuhn only served to formalize the split between the Bund and Hitler's Germany. Perhaps the Bund had become Americanized—perhaps it had always been. Certainly the disunion gave the rebels a clearer cause, so to speak. Lacking the political muscle or membership necessary to either establish or maintain independence, the Bund continued to live under the shadow of Hitler's swastika.

ENDNOTES
Chapter 5

1. Weekly papers were published in New York, Philadelphia, Chicago, and Los Angeles. Proposed expansion would include Boston, Salt Lake City, Minneapolis, and Seattle. See *New York Times*, 20 March 1938.

2. Leland V. Bell, *In Hitler's Shadow: The Anatomy of American Nazism* (New York: Kennikat Press, 1973), p. 60.

3. On the same night of the Bund's mass rally in New York, representatives of various anti-Nazi organizations met in Carnegie Hall to protest the German dictatorship. Anti-Fascist sentiment was not solely in response to the Bund. During the period before World War II, a myriad of Fascist organizations operated in the United States. Individually their impact was insignificant. Viewed as a whole, however, they were quite threatening. For the purposes of this study, and because of the publicity afforded the Bund, anti-Fascist sentiment is equated to anti-Nazi feeling.

4. *New York Times*, 8 February 1938.

5. Ibid., 13 February 1938.

6. Ibid., 14 February 1938.

7. As noted, for instance, by the historian LaVern J. Rippley in his work *The German Americans* (Boston: Twayne Publishers, 1976), pp. 196-199. This fear comprised a desire for isolation, strict immigration quotas, and vigilance of fifth column invasion.

8. It must be acknowledged that anxiety over fifth column invasion was not without merit given the shifting in the balance of power occurring in Europe and Germany's attempts at subversion in the United States during World War I. For German spy activity in the United States see Ladislas Farago, *The Game of the Foxes: The Untold Story of German Espionage in the United States and Great Britain*

during World War II (New York: David McKay Company, Inc., 1971); Alton Frye, *Nazi Germany and the American Hemisphere* (New Haven: Yale University Press, 1967); Gerhard L. Weinberg, *The Foreign Policy of Hitler's Germany, 1933-1936* (Chicago: University of Chicago Press, 1971).

9. LaVern Rippley, *The German Americans*, p. 199.

10. See O. John Rogge, *The Official German Report* (New York: Thomas Yoseloff, 1961), pp. 56-57. Also U. S. Congress, House, 77th Congress, 1st Session, Special Committee on Un-American Activities. *Investigation of Un-American Propaganda Activities in the United States*. House Report No. 1. January 3, 1941, p. 5.

11. For a complete discussion of Manfred Zapp, the German Library of Information, and the German Railroads Information Office, see O. John Rogge, *The Official German Report*, pp. 68-82; and Alton Frye, *Nazi Germany and the American Hemisphere*, pp. 80-101.

12. In June 1941, the U. S. government halted its publication and the journal was removed from the libraries. See LaVern Rippley, *The German Americans*, p. 202.

13. See, for example, Henry Hoke, *Black Mail* (New York: Readers Book Service, Inc., 1944).

14. The best discussions of Hitler's views regarding the United States are by Saul Frielander, *Prelude to Downfall: Hitler and the United States 1939-1941* (New York: Alfred A. Knopf, Inc., 1967); James V. Compton, *The Swastika and the Eagle: Hitler, the United States, and the Origins of World War II* (Boston: Houghton Mifflin Co., 1967); and Alton Frye, *Nazi Germany and the American Hemisphere*, pp. 168-185.

15. First and foremost in Nazi ideology is the belief, aptly stated by Dennis Prager and Joseph Telushkin in *Why the Jews? The Reasons for Antisemitism* (New York: Simon and Schuster, Inc., 1983), that the Nazis did not persecute the Jews to gain power, but gained power to persecute the Jews. This doctrine would not be altered for any purpose, not even by the winning of World War II.

16. United States Department of State, *Documents on German Foreign Policies, 1918-1945, from the Archives of the German Foreign Ministry* (Washington, D. C.: USGPO, 1949-1950), Series C, Volume II, pp. 640-641. Hereafter cited as DGFP. Dieckhoff's career and contributions to German foreign policy is highlighted in Warren F. Kimball, "Dieckhoff and America: A German's View of German-American Relations, 1937-1941," *The Historian* 27/2 (1965): 218-243.

17. Ronald W. Johnson, "German American Bund and Nazi Germany, 1936-1941," *Studies in History and Society* 6/2 (1975): 33.

18. DGFP, D, I, pp. 632-633.

19. Ibid., pp. 635-638.

20. Ibid., p. 658. "Nazintern" was coined by Winston Churchill in his denunciation of the AO. See Donald M. McKale, *The Swastika Outside Germany* (Ohio: The Kent State University Press, 1977), p. 130.

21. DGFP, D, I, p. 650.

22. Ibid., pp. 709, 711.

23. Ibid., pp. 664-677.

24. Ibid.

25. Ibid.

26. Donald McKale, *The Swastika Outside Germany*, p. 142.

27. DGFP, D, I, pp. 692-693.

28. *New York Times*, 1 March 1938.

29. Ibid.

30. U. S. Department of State, *Foreign Relations of the United States 1938* (Washington, D. C.: USGPO, 1955), Volume II, pp. 461-462.

31. *New York Times*, 1 March 1938.

32. Ibid, and *Time* 14 March 1938, pp. 15-16.

33. *New York Times*, 2 March 1938.

34. Ibid.

35. Ibid.

36. Ibid.

37. DGFP, D, IV, pp. 701-702.

38. Ibid., D, I, pp. 664-678.

39. Ibid., D, IV, p. 650.

40. Ibid.

41. Bund Command 18, 3 May 1938.

42. Ibid.

43. Ibid.

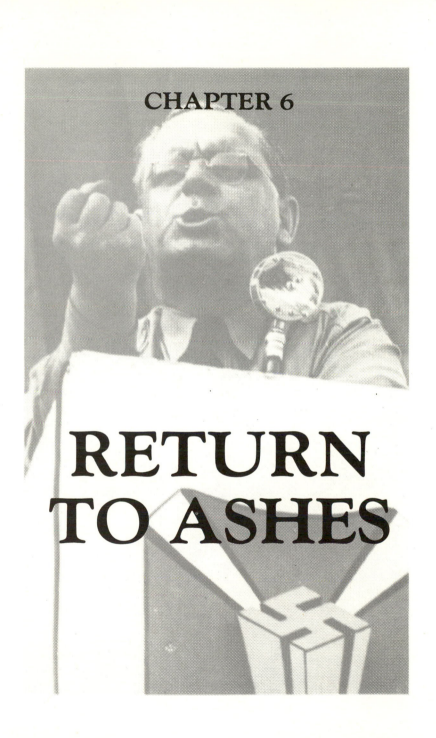

CHAPTER 6

RETURN TO ASHES

CHAPTER 6

RETURN TO ASHES

In May 1938, House Resolution 282, which authorized the formation of the House Committee to Investigate Un-American Activities, was passed by a vote of 191-41.[1] Congress' investigative arm was once again called forth to do that which no other federal agency was empowered—to assess Americanism. Fathered by Samuel Dickstein and chaired by Martin Dies, a strident isolationist and anti-immigrationist from Texas, the House Un-American Activities Committee, or Dies Committee as it came to be called, symbolized America's commitment to democratic purism.[2] It also symbolized Martin Dies' desire for social justice, as he saw it, and became a general expression of his ardent, perhaps xenophobic, nationalism. As he loudly purported:

> The experience of this generation, more than that of any other, has demonstrated that the enemies within a country constitute a peril as great as any foe. Treason from within, aided by invasion from without, has been responsible for the speed with which modern governments have collapsed in the face of totalitarian assaults. Stalin and Hitler have pushed their Trojan Horse tactics to the point of perfection . . . Indeed, the Trojan Horse, as we have seen, has been drawn into labor

organizations, political parties, peace societies, educational institutions, civic clubs, and
even into the government itself.[3]

Representative Dies was determined not to let this
"infiltration" go any further. Buoyed by public opinion
and braced by a majority of his colleagues, Dies' fervor
proved appealing. His stance was an attractive call to
arms—it had patriotic panache and carried the
masses. Only a faint caution on its potential for
extremism was sounded. Once again Representative
Maury Maverick, also of Texas, warned that such an
investigation would only engender race hatred while it
obtained headlines for the committee members. Fear-
ing side show behavior on the part of the committee,
Maverick advised that, in his view, it would be of more
use to investigate unemployment or inequalities in the
South than to foment unrest over alleged un-American
activity.[4]

Madison Square Garden Rally, February 20, 1939

*George Washington display at the
massive rally in February, 1939*

For the second time, Representative Maverick's
caveat went unheeded. The Dies Committee was
appropriated $25,000 to conduct an investigation
which Congressman Dies maintained would take only
7 months. The committee launched itself into the
examination of:

> (1) the extent, character, and objects of un-
> American propaganda activities in the Uni-
> ted States, (2) the diffusion within the United

George Washington Birthday Rally leaflet

178

States of subversive and un-American propaganda that is instigated from foreign countries or of a domestic origin and attacks the principle of the form of government as guaranteed by the Constitution, and (3) all other questions in relation thereto that would aid Congress in any necessary remedial legislation.[5]

For the next two years the Bund fought stridently for its life. Although the formation of the Committee went virtually unnoticed by the group, its significance was not lost on the general public. Confident that such federal attention would certainly right the prevalent wrongs, America anxiously backed her government in its clean-up campaign. In anticipation, the leading press organs, including the *New York Times*, Los Angeles *Times*, and Chicago *Tribune*, intensified their coverage of the Bund and chronicled as well the respondent rise in anti-Nazi activity.[6]

Although the Bund did not immediately respond to this obvious threat to its existence, German America did. Fellow Germanic organizations became apprehensive of a possible impact upon their livelihood as a result of this federal action and moved to minimize it. On 4 July 1938, the New York Organization of German and Hungarian Veterans of World War I deleted the word "Bund" from its title, wishing to avoid the stigma of pro-Fascism or the possibility of an association with the Bund.[7] The League of German Culture, a social and cultural society, sought similar disassociation through an open proclamation of devotion to the American democratic system.[8] It, too, hastened to avoid the consequences of the stereotype presented by the Bund. Going a step further, in open disavowal, the New York German-American Conference, an established, conservative coalition of social groups, informed Kuhn that the Bund would not be invited to participate in the 1938 traditional annual German Day Celebration.[9]

Already isolated from Germany, and now from much of German America, the Bund, for once, appeared vulnerable. Sensing this, local authorities moved in to disable the movement on legal grounds. Bund operations everywhere were subjected to intense scrutiny, and often prosecution, as local, civil, and law enforcement agencies began monitoring the Bund's activities. While adherence to National Socialism was not a crime in itself, sufficient laws governing the group's social privileges could be called into play, thus making the group's existence difficult if not impossible.

The first significant legal suit brought against the Bund was the Riverhead Case in July 1938.[12] On trial were six officials of the German American Settlement League, one of the Bund's ancillary corporations, on suspicion of representing an oath-bound organization—the Bund. If the allegation could be proven, the German-American Settlement League could be found guilty on the basis of a law requiring all oath-bound organizations to submit a membership roster to the New York Secretary of State. A guilty verdict held not only the promise of imposed fines and/or imprisonment for the officials, but highly unfavorable publicity for the group as well. The portent of a finding of guilt was dissolution of the Bund.

The trial itself was anything but landmark. The prosecution's case rested on the testimony of former Nazi Willy Brandt who swore that when he joined the Bund in May 1938, he was required to pledge his allegiance to Adolf Hitler and the Bund hierarchy. The defense consisted of twenty-five Bundists, including James Wheeler-Hill, National Secretary of the Bund,

Madison Square Garden Rally

all of whom testified that an oath was not required for membership and that Brandt had been denied membership to the Bund.[11] For the most part, testimony was markedly suspect—the prosecution rested its case solely upon the testimony of one man with admitted questionable integrity. Regardless, the abrasive

Rally in Madison Square Garden, February 20, 1935

behavior and virulently anti-Semitic attitude of the
Bund defendants so shocked the jury that they deliber-
ated only fifteen minutes before handing down a guilty
verdict. Clearly it was the existence of the German
American Bund, rather than the lesser issue of regis-
tration procedures, that was on trial.

Costs of such litigation sapped Bund resources. The
organization was not financially equipped to cover
extensive legal expenses. A "fighting fund" was
created by Kuhn immediately upon conclusion of the
trial to solicit money from the membership to pay legal
costs, but members could not, or would not, carry the
entire financial burden.[12] Equally important, adverse
court activity cost the Bund prestige and membership.
Its vulnerabilities were on public display, which
strengthened the opposition and weakened the
movement.

Although Kuhn had warned his organization of a
hostile public as he admonished them to welcome every
fight, neither he nor his organization was prepared for
the onslaught directed against them at all levels.[13]

Local and state governments tore the foundation out from under the Bund by concentrating on specific operational aspects of the organization. Legal authority to sell beer and wine at recreational camps was subject to local ordinance as was the wearing of uniforms and maintenance of the OD.[14] Application of legal sanction drove away membership, undercut the group's financial stability, and further aroused an already suspicious public. Clearly, "local and state police powers, ordinances and legislation can harass any group obnoxious to the overwhelming majority of the community."[15]

Decimation of the group was not readily apparent to observers, however, owing for the most part to the dedication and tenacity of the Bund leadership. Kuhn

Astoria unit of the Bund, 1939

Fritz Kuhn addressing a rally

cried persecution and the organization followed, content to make martyrs of their fallen comrades. Throughout the spring and summer the Bund was ceaselessly active. None of the organization's activities was suspended; gatherings and rallies continued; and recreational camps flourished as the general membership sought comfort among their own.

While the group attempted to parry local and state attacks, federal action got underway when formal hearings before the House Un-American Activities Committee (HUAC) opened in Washington, D. C., on 12 August. Dies set the stage for his Committee in his introductory statement when he declared:

> . . . this committee is determined to conduct its investigation upon a dignified plane and

to adopt and maintain throughout the course of the hearings a judicial attitude. The committee has no preconceived views of what the truth is respecting the subject matter of this inquiry . . . We shall be fair and impartial at all times and treat every witness with fairness and courtesy . . . The Chair wishes to emphasize that the committee is more concerned with facts than with opinions, and with specific proof than with generalities . . . In investigating un-American activities it must be borne in mind that because we do not agree with opinions or philosophies of others does not necessarily make such opinions or philosophies un-American.[16]

February 22, 1939, Los Angeles Bund meeting,

Thus, Dies himself set the standard upon which his Committee would be judged. To be sure, it was a lofty set of principles under which to work—a set of principles Dies found impossible to maintain.[17] Given the temper of the times and the fierce nationalism which reigned throughout the course of the hearings, total objectivity was not a reasonably attainable goal. While Dies and his fellow committee members, given the benefit of all doubts, strove to carry out what they considered to be their patriotic duty, they found it difficult to control their rage and desperation when actually faced with hostile Bundists. Faced with the personages of Fascism or communism, Dies especially tended to give in to the emotions of the hunter and

Members of the OD (Security Service)
at the February Rally, 1939

unfortunately carried the Committee. While the Bund was far from lily-white, the Committee's questioning was often openly fraught with bias. Testimony was manipulated to confirm the suspicious activity which the committee was dedicated to find. Moreover, although most of the hearings were conducted in relative privacy, photographers and members of the press were allowed entry, and given the subject matter and Dies' zealotry, the "copy" was good. The public had only to turn on their radios or read their newspapers to keep abreast of investigative events.

The first witness before the Dies Committee was John C. Metcalfe, a German-born former reporter for the Chicago *Daily Times* who had infiltrated the Bund

The OD (Security Force) at Camp Siegfried, c. 1939

in 1937.[18] As an investigator for the HUAC, Metcalfe had joined the Astoria, Queens, unit as Helmut Oberwinder. Extremely successful in his assimilation into the group, Metcalfe was able to provide the Committee with previously unknown operational procedures while confirming generally-held opinions on such popular particulars as the salute, the swastika, and the OD. His testimony, embellished with stories of Kuhn's iron-handed direction, concentrated on the activities of the Bund and its connection with the Third Reich, and conformed to prevalent preconceptions of German control and dominance. Metcalfe named the Bund as the backbone of the Hitler movement and charged that the "foreign institute of the Nazis is actively engaged in directing, planning, and helping to finance under various names the activities and programs of the German-American Bund in the United States."[19]

Virtually all of the first day's testimony was devoted to the Bund which set the stage for later examinations of National Socialist propaganda. Metcalfe was followed on the stand by Peter Gissibl, one of the founders of Teutonia and head of the Bund's Chicago unit, who echoed Metcalfe's charges and stated unequivocally that he had severed relations with the Bund over differences with Kuhn concerning anti-Jewish policies.[20]

Following this initial testimony, however, Fascist groups were dropped for the rest of the year as the Committee focused on communism. Never losing its initial fervor, the Committee's activities were carried in the leading presses accompanied by excerpts of pertinent testimony. The calibre of this testimony, however, drew mixed reactions. While a good deal of honest, corroborated testimony was heard and reported, enough of it was so flagrantly unsubstantiated and sensational as to draw a denunciation from President Roosevelt.[21] Not so from the American public, however.

A Gallup Poll held just before the hearings' recess on 15 December 1938, showed three out of five voters were familiar with the work of the Committee, and three out of four of those who knew of it believed it should be continued.[22] Moreover, the *Washington Post* lauded Dies as the unequalled winner of the "Americanism award for 1938" as a result of his "outstanding patriotic service."[23]

Kuhn took heed of the Committee's efforts as well. Hardly unaware of the political ramifications of all

Fritz Kuhn and August Klapprott, 1939

that had transpired during the year, Kuhn rallied his movement at the German American Bund National Convention which opened on 3 September.[24] Speaking to a crowd of 632 delegates assembled at New York City's Turnhalle for the national officer elections, Kuhn first categorically, although cryptically, denied Germany had disavowed either him or the movement:

> Comrades, concerning this trip to Germany I cannot and may not say and report very much. Here I must absolutely request your confidence. I tell you only this much, that had my trip been without success, or had I unfavorable reports to make, I would not be standing before you today, but would have withdrawn my constituency . . .[25]

That particular question disposed of, Kuhn and his delegates began an analysis of the organization and its trials. The ensuing debates were surprisingly candid.

Bundists gathered at Camp Nordland, 1939

There was no effort on the part of the leadership to gloss over the problems confronting the movement. Their inability to attract further German American support; diminished economic strength; and rivalries existing between the OD, Youth Division, and Prospective Citizens League were among those topics frankly discussed.[26] Although faced with debilitating difficulties, there was no motion to capitulate or surrender existing principles. The Bund remained true to itself, rallying to its own defense and endorsing Kuhn as national leader. As has been noted, these annual conventions were held both as spiritual retreats and leadership checks. Here was an opportunity for the representatives of the various districts to either show their support of Kuhn and his activities or vote in a replacement.

Kuhn received the vote of confidence, though some accommodation was adopted. Another survival-oriented move was made to further "Americanize" the movement. The Bund emerged from the convention with a new eight-point "American" program designed to ensure the continued existence of the organization. The Bund proclaimed itself in favor of:[27]

1. A socially just, white, Gentile-ruled United States.
2. Gentile-controlled labor unions free from Jewish, Moscow-directed domination.
3. Gentiles in all positions of importance in government, national defense, and educational institutions.
4. Severance of diplomatic relations with Soviet Russia, outlawing of the Communist Party in the United States.
5. Immediate cessation of the dumping of all political refugees on the shores of the United States.

6. Thorough cleansing of the Hollywood film industries of all alien, subversive doctrines.
7. Cessation of all abuse of the freedom of the pulpit, press, radio and stage.
8. A return of our Government to the policies of George Washington. Aloofness from foreign entanglements. Severance of all connections with the League of Nations.

Such a program voiced some concerns popular with isolationists throughout the country. With emphasis on the eradication of the Communist threat, the Bund hoped to blend its particular program with already prevalent sentiment. A greater effort would be made to recruit Americans into the movement, delegates were advised to use the term "white man" frequently, to use English at rallies and in publications, and seek alliances with right-wing societies.[28] Once again the Bund attempted to camouflage its National Socialism in what it perceived to be Americanisms.

The effort failed. Once again the Bund launched a campaign so repugnantly pro-New Germany that the cloak of Americanism went unnoticed. Following the convention, a mass rally which attracted some two thousand was held at Camp Nordland, New Jersey, where the Bund put on a bombastic show of race hatred and ardent National Socialism in an effort to present a strong, unified front and attract recruits.[29] Later that month, as Hitler came away from the Munich Conference carrying Czechoslovakia in his pocket, the Bund lauded his diplomatic victory, peppering its press with praise for the man they claimed championed the cause of liberty.[30] Their elation was hardly matched by most Americans. Skeptical of the accord and fearful of the increased German militancy, the American public viewed the Bund's reaction as further proof of its ties to

Posting a guard at Camp Nordland, 1939

Germany. In Union City, New Jersey, on 2 October, a crowd of nearly five thousand gathered in front of the hall where Kuhn was scheduled to speak. The meeting was cancelled after a number of them broke into the building and began to fight with Bundists. In Newark, with similar hostility, a crowd attacked Bundists coming from another of their meetings. Anti-Nazis picketed Bund meetings and assembled en masse at Bund

gatherings crying their denunciations of the organization and responding to German aggression with violence of their own.[31]

Despite this uproar the Bund marched on. In strict
defense of Germany's policies, it again contradicted its
newly proclaimed Americanism in its response to
Hitler's first organized Jewish pogrom, the *Kristall-
nacht*, in November 1938. As America reeled in disbe-
lief and revulsion, the Bund stood steadfast, making no
apologies for Hitler's barbarity. Comparing the assas-
sination of the German embassy's third secretary by a
Jew to attacks on Bund meetings by anti-Nazis, Bundists argued that the resultant pogrom was a justifiable
act of retribution.[32] This open endorsement of an event
as yet unprecedented in cruelty and inhumanity furthered the hostility aimed at the Bund and caused even
the most prestigious German American organization,
the Steuben Society, to repudiate it.[33]

Seemingly unperturbed by the rising antagonism
directed against it, the Bund continued to display both
arrogance and a strong belief in its inherent rightness.
The American scene, the Bund believed, was just a
variation of the environment Hitler had been faced
with a decade earlier. Comparing its struggles and
difficulties with those encountered by the NSDAP in
its nascent years, the Bund never faltered in its conviction. Buoying the membership with dreams of Hitler's
ultimate victory and the resultant greatness of the New
Germany, Kuhn and the Bund leadership urged their
followers to endure the hard times despite their martyrdom. And, in celebration of what Bundists were sure
would be eventual triumph, the German American
Bund organized a massive show of solidarity and
unity.

On 20 February 1939, America witnessed a grand

display of American National Socialism as the German American Bund presented the Pro-American Rally and George Washington Birthday Exercises. It was a massive show of strength. Madison Square Garden was filled to capacity with attendance estimated at more than 20,000.[34] A two-block perimeter had been cordoned off in anticipation of a counter-demonstration, and more than 2,000 New York policemen were on hand to answer the anticipated violence. Inside, the hall was resplendent with American flags and a larger-than-life poster of George Washington hung behind the podium. Positioned on the platform were the flags of the United States, Italy, Germany, and the German American Bund. The aisles were lined with OD men. The Bund's national leadership was present, and speakers included J. Wheeler-Hill, the Bund's National Secretary; the Reverend S. G. Van

Color Guard and OD (Security Force) at Camp Nordland, 1939

Bosse, a minister from Philadelphia; George Froebese, Mid-Western Department Leader; Rudolf Markmann, Eastern Department Leader; G. Wilhelm Kunze, National Public Relations Director; and Fritz Kuhn. These officers of the Bund arose to glorify America and condemn the racial amalgamation which had occurred since George Washington's time. Anti-Semitism and racial mongrelization were major themes. All speeches were given in English to a crowd that rocked the great hall with sharply punctuated cheers of "Free America!"[35]

Kuhn spoke last. During his speech he categorically denied German sponsorship and heartily denounced Jewish influence in America. The crowd suddenly rose to its feet and roared in anger. A young man, Isadore Greenbaum, had broken through the lines of OD men to rush at Kuhn.[36] Greenbaum was knocked down by a dozen troopers and badly beaten before the police ushered him to relative safety. Shielded by his protective arm, Kuhn resumed his presentation. Order was restored, the rally concluded, and Bundists exited the hall to find the New York police force protecting them from an angry mob of approximately 100,000.[37]

That single rally and the perceptions taken away by the press confirmed public suspicion that the Bund was an intense, dedicated, and thoroughly organized group of German Americans devoted to Kuhn and the National Socialist philosophy.[38] The public outcry that followed the rally was intense. Media coverage in both national and international tribunes prompted Germany, this time emphatically, to "officially disclaim any connection with the German-American Bund."[39]

Like the projection of the Thousand-Year Reich, however, there seemed no foreseeable end to the Bund's mysterious wellspring of energy. Though anti-Nazi activity had increased to a level equal with that of the Bund, and the Dies Committee loomed high in America's expectations, still the phoenix flew high and strong. Although the Bund was not, in reality, the politically strong or dangerous organization that general perception had made it, it appeared invincible.

Whether the Bund could have, given the circumstances, survived the war, will remain open to debate. Anti-Nazi activity had served not only to draw further

Bund rally at Camp Nordland, 1939
(Fritz Kuhn 4th from right, August Klapprott to his left)

Outdoor rally at Camp Nordland, 1939

attention to the group, but had mobilized domestic forces against it. In the end, however, it was neither vigorous community effort nor the Dies Committee which forced the phoenix home—rather an administrative matter of fiscal accountability.

In March 1939, an inquiry was launched to investigate the Bund's financial activities to ascertain whether it had paid New York City taxes on the sale of National Socialist paraphernalia.[40] Organized by Mayor Fiorello H. LaGuardia and District Attorney Thomas E. Dewey, agents of this Special Tax Emergency Investigation broke into Bund headquarters and seized the movement's records. On the basis of evidence thus collected, the investigation began. Sessions were conducted in private, and Kuhn was called for frequent testimony.[41] Meanwhile, the Bund continued its activities. On 21 April, the Bund hosted a Birthday Party Rally for Adolf Hitler at Ebling's Casino in the

Bronx. Approximately eight hundred attended, including one hundred and thirty nonuniformed OD.[42] The rally was heavily guarded by police, and speakers limited their exhortations to the salvation of Christendom rather than to anti-Semitism. The high point of the rally was the reading, by Kuhn, of a telegram sent to Hitler by the movement. It read:

> To the greatest German, the liberator and protector of the Reich, Adolf Hitler, who showed to all Aryan people the way to freedom, on his fiftieth birthday: victory and hail. The German American Bund in New York.[43]

In May, Fritz Kuhn was indicted on charges of theft of a total of $14,548 of Bund funds. His passport was immediately confiscated and he was later arrested in Krumsville, near Allentown, Pennsylvania.[44]

Despite the indictment by the New York Grand Jury, Kuhn was re-elected *Bundesfuehrer* of the German American Bund at a closed convention at New York's Turnhalle in July. The 550 delegates present maintained that according to the leadership principle, Kuhn's use of the organization's funds was implicitly approved by the group and could not, therefore, be considered larceny.[45] Kuhn had committed no crime against the Bund in the eyes of its members. The fact that he was indicted and arrested only further alienated the group from the broader society and encouraged feelings of martyrdom. Clearly, they believed, they were victims of discrimination based upon their nationality and beliefs.

The leadership grant which Kuhn accepted had become a hollow position by that time. Ever increasing harassment of the organization and of its members by numerous investigations and the impending European

war caused a significant exodus from the Bund, especially among the old guard.[46] Their departure precipitated a breakdown in the chain of command. Some left
the movement outright, frustrated in their efforts to
build a National Socialist party in the United States,
others merely withdrew moral and financial support.
Those that left had constituted the bureaucracy
through which the leadership principle operated. Their
replacements lacked their dedication and tenacity, and
the movement began to crumble from within. Despite
Kuhn's claims of German support, none was forthcoming, nor was there a call from Hitler beckoning his
disciples home. The Bund was not strong enough to
withstand the scrutiny and subsequent intolerance
levied by a frightened public, and it began to
disintegrate.

On 16 August, almost anticlimactically, Fritz Kuhn
appeared before the Dies Committee.[47] During his two-
day appearance, Kuhn brought little in the way of new
evidence, but did produce a sensational show. He was
clearly upset, highly defiant, and extremely defensive.
He closely matched the emotional tenor of his counter-
parts on the Committee. The resultant sparks provided
flame for the attending press. Kuhn's examination
consisted largely of exchanges of shouted accusations
by Committee members and roaring denials from
Kuhn. Police intervention was required in one instance
to prevent a violent encounter between Kuhn and
Representative Starnes.[48]

Adding fuel to the already consuming fire, Kuhn was
followed on the stand by Helen Vooros, a former
member of the Bund's youth group. Committee
members sat entranced as she described in detail the
workings of the youth movement and her group's trip
to Germany. She cited Germany's objectives:

Nazi Germany would get back all the territory lost in the World War, including Czecho-Slovakia, Danzig and the Polish Corridor, Schleswig-Holstein and the German colonies. Then it would take over Scandinavia. After that it would capture the United States because of the large content of German blood among its citizens.[49]

Her group was admonished to "work hard and strive to become school teachers because in such positions they could most effectively promote the Nazi program."[50] Miss Vooros' testimony chronicled Bund indoctrination techniques and German interest and guidance in and of the group during their pilgrimage.[51] The headlines were given, however, to her cries of sexual harassment while on board ship. Her testimony's overall accuracy cancelled any questions of irrelevance.

Outdoor rally at Camp Nordland, 1939

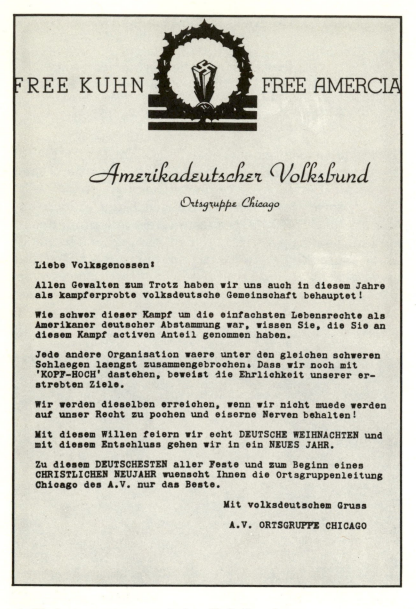

FREE KUHN   FREE AMERCIA

Amerikadeutscher Volksbund

Ortsgruppe Chicago

Liebe Volksgenossen:

Allen Gewalten zum Trotz haben wir uns auch in diesem Jahre
als kampferprobte volksdeutsche Gemeinschaft behauptet!

Wie schwer dieser Kampf um die einfachsten Lebensrechte als
Amerikaner deutscher Abstammung war, wissen Sie, die Sie an
diesem Kampf activen Anteil genommen haben.

Jede andere Organisation waere unter den gleichen schweren
Schlaegen laengst zusammengebrochen. Dass wir noch mit
'KOPF-HOCH' dastehen, beweist die Ehrlichkeit unserer er-
strebten Ziele.

Wir werden dieselben erreichen, wenn wir nicht muede werden
auf unser Recht zu pochen und eiserne Nerven behalten!

Mit diesem Willen feiern wir echt DEUTSCHE WEIHNACHTEN und
mit diesem Entschluss gehen wir in ein NEUES JAHR.

Zu diesem DEUTSCHESTEN aller Feste und zum Beginn eines
CHRISTLICHEN NEUJAHR wuenscht Ihnen die Ortsgruppenleitung
Chicago des A.V. nur das Beste.

                    Mit volksdeutschem Gruss

                        A.V. ORTSGRUPPE CHICAGO

A Christmas message urging Kuhn's release

The press fed the unsavory accounts to a hungry public.[52]

There were further hearings on the Bund throughout the fall, but for the most part they were sporadic as the Committee turned its attention leftward. Except for the sensation that Bundists irrevocably engendered, there was very little evidence to be had. Kuhn was called back once more on 19 October for a five hour session characterized by the bickering which had become typical.[53] During questioning the Committee valiantly and unceasingly attempted to determine the Bund's relationships with other ultra-right groups such as the Christian Front and William Pelley's Silver Shirts. The Committee assumed the existence of a united front. Kuhn heartily denied this, but to no avail. The Committee's mind was made up.

All of this proved to be inconsequential for the Bund. Kuhn's indictment by the New York Grand Jury had sounded the death knell for the Bund. The possibility of a lengthy imprisonment moved Kuhn to appoint a successor. At a closed meeting of the OD held in Ebling's Casino in the Bronx, Kuhn named Gerhard Wilhelm Kunze, former National Public Relations Director and Deputy *Fuehrer*, to carry on the fight.[54] Though seemingly optimistic and confident before the gathering of 1,200, Kuhn could not have failed to have grasped the gravity of his—and the organization's—circumstances.

Kuhn was tried and convicted of grand larceny in November.[55] Sentenced to two and a half to five years in Sing Sing prison, his incarceration was front page news in the *Weckruf* which screamed, "Kuhn a Prisoner of War!"[56] Bund members were angered and frustrated at the injustice of the decision, yet there was no great cry to action. The movement began to splinter

and disintegrate as the leadership principle broke
down.[57] The Bund was well along its transit from
zenith to nadir. Rocked with dissension and plagued
with increasing investigations, financial collapse and
spiritual breakdown, the Bund—like the legendary
phoenix—had begun its descent to the ashes of its
origin.

The Bund had reached its peak under Kuhn, and
rapidly lost momentum after his indictment. On 6
December, the day after Kuhn went to prison, the
Bund's executive committee met and deposed him.
Kunze now took the reins and the movement sustained
itself, but as only a shell of its former self. For all
intents and purposes, the Bund ceased to exist with
Kuhn's internment. Mention of the group in the newspapers virtually halted, and the Dies Committee, con-

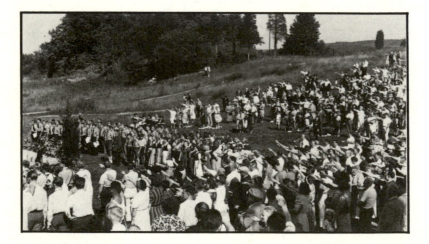

Bundists celebrating at Camp Nordland, 1939

tinuing its investigations, concentrated on the Communist party and other left-wing organizations.

Under the leadership of Fritz Kuhn, the Bund had formed and grown into an organization which impacted upon two continents. Under the National Socialist philosophy, he was the Bund leader, and the Bund and the leader were one and the same. Kuhn's incarceration and the rapid deterioration of the organization which followed were cause and effect; the Bund and Kuhn could not be separated without the collapse of the former. The effort that remained under Kunze was a shadow movement which daily grew smaller as public censure and pressure increased. On 8 December 1941, the day after Pearl Harbor, what was left of the executive committee met and voted to disband the movement. The plummet of the phoenix was complete.

ENDNOTES
Chapter 6

1. Objective studies on the methodology, procedure, and overall effectiveness of the Dies Committee include those by Robert K. Carr, *The House Committee on Un-American Activities* (New York: Cornell University Press, 1952); Walter Goodman, *The Committee* (New York: Farrar, Straus and Giroux, 1968); and August Raymond Ogden, *The Dies Committee: A Study of the Special House Committee for the Investigation of Un-American Activities, 1938-1944* (Washington, D. C.: The Catholic University of America Press, 1945).

2. Martin Dies' first action upon election to Congress in 1931 was to introduce a bill which would have provided for the suspension of general immigration into the Untied States for five years.

3. Martin Dies, *The Trojan Horse in America* (New York: Dodd, Mead and Co., 1940), p. 348.

4. As quoted in Ogden, *The Dies Committee*, p. 44.

5. Ibid., p. 43. The original members of the Committee were Martin Dies (TX), Arthur D. Healey (MA), John J. Dempsey (NM), Joe Starnes (AL), Harold G. Mosier (OH), Noah M. Mason (IL), and J. Parnell Thomas (NJ). The number of committee members was increased to eight in 1943.

6. By far, the Committee's emphasis centered on communism. However, for the purposes of this study, comments are limited to its study of Fascism. There were notable journals that reported accurately, and indeed were highly uncomplimentary of the Committee, for example, the Washington *Post*, St. Louis *Post-Dispatch*, and the *New Republic*.

7. *New York Times*, 4 July 1938.

8. Ibid., 16 April 1938.

9. Ibid., 15 September 1938.

10. Leland V. Bell, *In Hitler's Shadow: The Anatomy of American Nazism* (New York: Kennikat Press, 1973), pp. 70-71.

11. *New York Times*, 7, 8, 12, 13 July 1938.

12. Ibid., 14 November 1939.

13. As Kuhn's experiences would show, it would be legal difficulties, rather than federal investigative action, that would break the back of the Bund. See Martha Glaser, "The German American Bund in New Jersey," *New Jersey History* 1974 92(1): 33-49.

14. For instance, Mayor LaGuardia of New York issued an order on 27 February 1939, banning uniformed guards. See the *New York Times*, 21 April 1939.

15. Martha Glaser, "The German American Bund in New Jersey," p. 33.

16. U. S. Congress, House, 75th Congress, 3rd Session, Special Committee to Investigate Un-American Activities and Propaganda in the United States, *Hearings*, Vol. I (Washington, D. C.: 1938). As quoted in Ogden, *The Dies Committee*, pp. 50-51; and Goodman, *The Committee*, p. 27.

17. For a critical review of the Dies Committee, see Goodman, *The Committee*; and Ogden, *The Dies Committee*.

18. Metcalfe's testimony found in U. S. Congress, House, 75th Congress, 3rd Session, Special Committee to Investigate Un-American Activities and Propaganda in the United States, *Hearings*, Vol. I (Washington, D. C.: 1938), pp. 3-47, 86-90. See also the *Chicago Daily Times*, 13 September 1937, p. 12.

19. *New York Times*, 13 August 1938.

20. Ibid. It must be acknowledged, given Gissibl's former leadership position in Teutonia, that his change in heart may have been due to the circumstances in which he found himself.

21. *New York Times*, 26 October 1938.

22. Ibid., 11 December 1938.

23. *Washington Post*, January 1939.

24. Bund Commands 19 and 20, 12 July and 16 August 1938.

25. As quoted in O. John Rogge, *The Official German Report* (New York: Thomas Yoseloff, 1961), pp. 127-128.

26. *Minutes of the 1938 National Convention of the German-American Bund.* The author wishes to thank the offices of Representative William Dickinson (AL) from whom she was able to procure a photocopy of this document.

27. Ibid., p. 66.

28. Ibid., pp. 47-62, 70-81, 88-98.

29. *New York Times*, 5 September 1938.

30. *Deutscher Weckruf und Beobachter*, 6, 13, 27 October 1938.

31. *New York Times*, 2, 3, 16, 17, 27 October 1938.

32. *Deutscher Weckruf und Beobachter*, 17, 24 November 1938.

33. *New York Times*, 23 November 1938.

34. For an excellent first-hand account of the Madison Square Garden Rally see Alson J. Smith, "I Went to a Nazi Rally," *Christian Century* 56 (8 March 1939): 320-322.

35. "Six Addresses on the Aims and Purposes of the German American Bund, Delivered at Madison Square Garden, New York City, February 20, 1939." Pamphlet provided to the author by a former member of the Bund, printing data unknown.

36. Smith, "I Went to a Nazi Rally," p. 321.

37. Ibid.

38. *New York Times*, 24, 26 February 1939.

39. Ibid., 26 February 1939.

40. Ibid., 4 March 1939.

41. Ibid., 7, 10, 16 March and 10 May 1939.

42. Ibid., 21 April 1939.

43. Ibid.

44. Ibid., 13, 26, 27 May 1939. Kuhn was arrested while travelling to rallies in Milwaukee and Chicago. Police claimed he was in flight of the pending indictment. He was released a day later on $5,000 bond and proceeded immediately to the aforementioned rallies. Kuhn's bail was renegotiated in September 1939 to $50,000 in lieu of the growing fear that he would leave the country. The membership collected the bail, all from private contributions, and Kuhn was released on 7 October. See *New York Times*, 30 September 1939.

45. *New York Times*, 4 July 1939.

46. A society known as the *Kameradschaft USA*, which functioned under the AO under Ernst Wilhelm Bohle, was begun in 1938 and directed by Fritz Gissibl. Its purpose was to solicit Germans in America who were willing to return to Germany. Those in highest demand were Germans who had come to the United States following World War I, and those 250,000 who in 1940 had not yet applied for citizenship papers. Many who left the Bund were in this category and had been members since 1933. See Sander A. Diamond, *The Nazi Movement in the United States 1924-1941* (Ithaca: Cornell University Press, 1974), pp. 310-312 and Appendix V; LaVern J. Rippley, *The German-Americans* (New York: University Press of America, 1984), pp. 207-209; and Alton Frye, *Nazi Germany and the American Hemisphere* (New Haven: Yale University Press, 1967), pp. 89-90.

47. Fritz Kuhn's testimony found in *Hearings*, Vol. 6: 3705-3889.

48. *New York Times*, 17 August 1939.

49. Ibid., 19 August 1939.

50. Ibid.

51. Helen Vooros' testimony found in *Hearings*, Vol. 6: 3891-3960.

52. *New York Times*, 19 August 1939.

53. *Hearings*, Vol. 10: 6043-6124.

54. *New York Times*, 26 October 1939.

55. Ibid., 25 October 1939.

56. Ibid., 7 December 1939.

57. For example, Sander Diamond, in his comprehensive treatise *The Nazi Movement in the United States* claims that Gerhard Kunze (Public Relations Director and Deputy *Fuehrer*), Wilbur Keegan (Bund attorney), and August Klapprott (Director of Camp Nordland and Eastern District Leader) were aware that Kuhn had been embezzling and were plotting to eliminate him. Not only does such an accusation go against everything the Bund stood for, the leadership principle foremost, but all sources disavow it as well on the grounds that there was absolutely nothing to gain at the time.

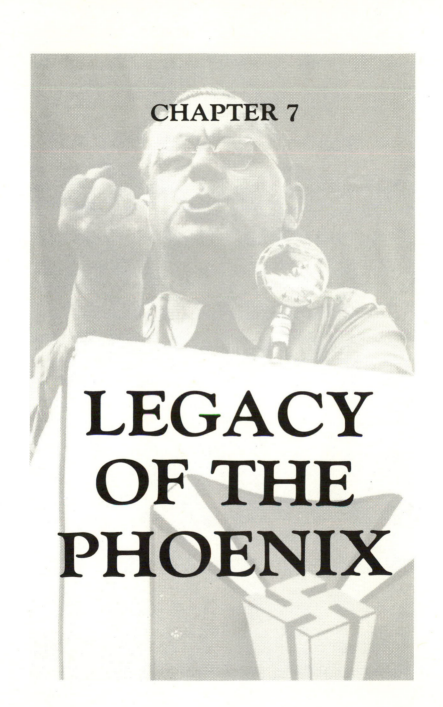

CHAPTER 7

LEGACY
OF THE
PHOENIX

CHAPTER 7

LEGACY OF THE PHOENIX

From 1936 to 1939, the German American Bund marched down American streets bedecked in Fascist regalia and proclaimed itself the spearhead of American purity and grandeur. Calling for the eradication of Communism and Judaism and maintenance of strict neutrality in the face of the upcoming world war, the Bund held itself up as the example of American might. The image presented was of fierce determination and unfailing conviction. The perception was of a dangerous and foreign radical organization.

During the 1930s, America witnessed the rise of many so-called radical groups. Splinter organizations of every hue and political cast emerged from an uncommitted national society. Under American law they were free to operate until such a time as they were seen as disruptive to commonly held tradition. Painfully emerging from the grip of the Great Depression only to be faced with the critical decision of international participation, the government of the United States provided the latitude for such expressions of variance and dissent. Indeed, the democratic principles under which the United States operates encouraged this freedom of criticism. In a society torn between traditional American isolationism and an emergent sense of global conscience, the Bund, as others created in this whirlpool of uncertainty, formed and moved easily.

It cannot be overly stressed, however, that the Bund was not born of Depression turbulence. The core of the German American Bund was well in place by 1929 in the form of the Teutonia Association. As has been shown, Teutonia comprised the chrysalis out of which the Bund emerged in 1936. Certainly it is debatable whether the Bund would have evolved had there been no Great Depression, but there is strong evidence to suggest that it drew its lifeblood from other sources.

First, there was a strong proclivity of German Americans to form cultural and social organizations. These organizations eased the assimilation process and helped guard against, while at the same time they encouraged, nativism.[1] When the German American Bund opened its doors to the membership, it did so professing a primal aim of preserving Germania. With its strong cultural and social auxiliaries, the Bund was able to capitalize on a heritage of German American fraternities.

Second, the treatment of German Americans during World War I and the aftermath of the Great War, especially in Germany, contributed substantially to the ability of the Bund to draw recruits. The German American community was deeply hurt by the harsh treatment it received during the war. A minority of this community reacted to the prejudice and scorn levied against them by retrenching into their Germanness. After World War I, new emigrants, bringing their nascent national socialism to American shores, would find a receptive audience by which to incorporate this doctrine into German American society.

Third, the German American Bund was a product of

Germany. It was initially comprised of German nationals who had survived World War I, its disastrous aftermath, and the social, political, and economic stresses present in Germany in the 1920s. These nationals echoed Adolf Hitler's discontent and had witnessed his transformations in their homeland. Once in America, they attempted to duplicate Hitler's efforts. While the German American Bund was neither financed by nor attached to the Third Reich, the Bund rested on organizations which had had the NSDAP stamp of approval. The German American Bund continually strove to gain that measure of approval. Those strivings brought about its downfall. While Bundists were Americans, they were also Germans. The group's resemblance to Hitler's Nazi movement went deeper than the uniforms, and even deeper than the ideology. All aspects of the organization were modelled on the German NSDAP. The leadership and youth groups made relatively regular pilgrimages to the New Germany in an effort to bring back as much of the dynamism and spirituality of the Nazi regime as could survive the transatlantic journey.

The intransigence of 1920s American society followed by the massive upheaval produced by the Great Depression most certainly provided the atmosphere which enabled the Bund to sustain itself as surely as it led to the growth of similarly-clad Fascist groups. But that is as far as the comparison can go. The German American Bund proposed a program and offered itself to the embrace of American society. However, the pomp and militancy of its uniformed OD backed up by an unceasing chorus of "Free America" sent no shivers of patriotic emotionalism down the spines of American on-lookers. Eventually the American populace passed judgement on the Bund's right to exist and mobilized

its national, state, and local forces to enforce its decision. This it did by a myriad of means, perhaps best
illustrated by the activities and decisions of the Dies
Committee.

As early as January 1939, the House Un-American
Activities Committee presented its findings on the status of un-Americanism in the United States. This it
continued to do annually throughout its tenure. Its
reports were, more often than not, merely summaries of
testimony heard throughout the course of the preceding year interjected with the committee's collective
opinion of whichever group it had previously singled
out to investigate. No new evidence was added; those
faithful followers who had monitored the Committee's
hearings through the press were not surprised at the
verdicts handed down in report form.

The Committee's initial judgement on the German
American Bund was included in its first report of 1939.
Summarizing the evidence collected from the first and
major witness against the Bund, John C. Metcalfe, the
Committee put forward a description of Kuhn's
National Socialist organization. Examining such
areas as the OD, correspondence and records, the
youth movement, and funds and propaganda, the
report provided a synopsis of Bund practice and doctrine and established the existence of "a relationship
. . . between the German Government and the German-
American Bund through the activities of Nazi Coun-
sels(sic) in this country."[2] All this was contrived on the
basis of testimony from one man. In fact, the supposi-
tion of a Bund-Reich conspiracy, as put forward by the
Committee, was based solely on Kuhn's boasts of
power made in an earlier conversation with the under-
cover agent, Metcalfe:

Fritz Kuhn

You see, I have a certain special arrangement with Hitler and Germany that whenever any of our groups have trouble with the
consulates in their districts that they are to
report it to me in full detail. I then take it up
with the Ambassador. Germany is not to be
troubled with it unless I get no satisfaction
from the Ambassador.[3]

Kuhn's claim was never substantiated and was, as has
been shown, generally negated by the content and tone
of diplomatic missives from the United States to Germany. The bravado was representative of Kuhn's fan-
ciful imagination and drive for importance. That he
would veer from the truth, and indeed lie, for the betterment of his organization or glorification of himself,
was apparent even to Reich ministries. Kuhn supplied

the Committee with information it was dedicated to find. However, the Committee's work was tainted by a predilection to take Kuhn at his word. Widespread and voluminous propaganda put out by Germany and filtered through all available channels, to include the consulates, only seemed to prove the connection. Kuhn's pompous flights of fancy, and the fact that "consuls and diplomatic representatives of Nazi Germany in this country show a much closer cooperation with the nationalists of their country than any other similar group accredited here" formed the foundation of the Committee's verdict.[4]

Also mentioned in the Committee's first report, and worthy of note in this study, was the German Bund. A wholly separate but similarly uniformed group headquartered in Chicago under the leadership of Dr. Frederick Draeger, the German Bund was characterized by the Committee as a bona fide Nazi organization.[5] Indeed, it was the branch of Hitler's NSDAP in America. No ties could be found between the German Bund and the German American Bund, nor was there any hint of an alliance as far as the Dies Committee was concerned, but it was the German American Bund, rather than the German Bund, which was singled out by the Committee and marked for un-Americanism.

The Committee continued its chronicle of the German American Bund and the rise of Fascist groups in general in its second annual report published in 1940.[6] Kuhn's testimony of the previous August was summarized and the administrative and organizational structure of the Bund repeated. In the report, Fritz Kuhn was heralded as an American Karl Henlein, and the Bund was likened to "Nazi groups which were built up in Austria and Czechoslovakia prior to their annexation by Germany."[7] The Committee went on to record the extent of Fascist activity across the country. Much of the report concentrated on relationships between the Bund and other rightist groups, such as the Christian Front and the Silver Shirt Legion of America, as the Committee attempted to prove the existence of a Fascist united front.[8] Proof of a right-wing coalition was evidenced by "the cooperation of certain other organizations with the German-American Bund."[9] "Other organizations" included the Silver Shirts, the American Rangers, Knights of the White Camellia, the Ku Klux Klan, the National Gentile League, the Christian Mobilizers, and others. This indictment was grounded on basis of the uniformity of the literature received and put out by the various groups, the fact that group leaders often addressed each other's rallies, and the relative commonality of the swastika.[12] To the Committee, those similarities smacked of collusion:

> The testimony which our committee has heard reveals a widespread cooperation between half a hundred of these Nazi-Fascist groups. Interchange of speakers and literature is common. On several occasions in recent months they have endeavored to come together in some kind of a permanent federation. So far these efforts have been frustrated by organizational jealousies, but the search for a "man on horseback" goes on.[11]

It was damning evidence regardless of its circumstantial nature. No documents were produced, nor testimony introduced by the leadership of any group so named, to indicate collusion of any kind. Certainly each group benefitted from any measure of publicity, negative or otherwise, given any so-called Fascist organization. But there is nothing to support any claims of united front or revolutionary activity insofar as the Bund is concerned.

The report abruptly concluded that the primary aims

of the Bund were the radical change in the American form of government and the collection of dues, and, in the opinion of the Committee:

> Examination of testimony and evidence received can only leave the committee with the conclusion that the German-American Bund must be classified with the Communist Party as an agent of a foreign government.
>
> Although at the present time it is difficult to establish the international ties of the Bund as clearly as in the case of the Communist Party, no reasonable person can read the testimony on the Bund and believe other than that the Bund is operating primarily in the interest of Germany.[12]

Although the Bund had lost all its vitality with Kuhn's incarceration, the Committee continued its hearings in October 1940, calling before it Gerhard Wilhelm Kunze, then *Bundesfuehrer*; August Klapprott, Eastern Department Leader and Director of Camp Nordland; and Richard W. Werner, a former Bundist turned informant.[13] While Kunze represented the Bund as a legitimate American organization whose main purpose was to protect the rights and prestige of German Americans, and Klapprott parried questions concerning a KKK rally held at Camp Nordland on 18 August 1940, Werner captivated the Committee with his assertion that the Bund was preparing itself for *Der Tag*, which would be necessarily prefaced by an over-throw of the United States' government. The Committee could not have asked for a more cooperative witness.

A final indictment of the German American Bund came in 1941 with the publication of the Committee's third annual report, and four months later, the publication of three Bund organizational documents.[14] The former was a broad condemnation of all National Socialist groups and their intent to subvert. The Committee, noting that the Bund had all but disintegrated, credited itself with smashing "that Nazi movement even before it was able to get under way."[15]

The organizational documents, secured from the Office of Gerhard Kunze, were the most concrete evidence presented to the Committee in its whole of testimony on the Bund. They comprised three documents produced by the Bund outlining basic organizational instructions for unit and branch directorates, the organic structure of the group, and the function and operation of the OD.[16] The manuscripts were highly specific, rigidly detailed, and reeked of the leadership principle. Although never directly stating German allegiance, the group's militant tone conclusively tied the German American Bund to Germany in the view of the Dies Committee.

For the most part, the Dies Committee merely voiced opinions and passed judgements that were shared, and indeed expected, by the American public. Commentators such as Walter Lippman, who compared the committee members to vigilantes, and William H. Kilpatrick, who called for the resignation of Martin Dies, were vocally in the minority.[17] The House Un-American Activities Committee had secured the mandate of the people and the judgements of this tribunal were accepted.[18]

The Dies Committee was formed to investigate un-American activities and dutifully went in search of subversion. This it did with great vigor. Guarding the national security against the threat of fifth column invasion, the Committee examined all personages and groups that fell into its self-made definition of un-

Americanism. It was looking for spies, acts of sabotage, popular front organizations, and individuals connected with foreign governments.[19] It found all those things, but, sadly, not necessarily because they were there.

The case of the German American Bund is a prime example. Its public image and the perception of strength and German backing that it strove so hard to radiate, with great success, was enough to "prove" its participation in un-American activities. And here lies the inherent evil of a committee designed to seek out "un-Americanism." Had the Dies Committee limited itself to the assertion that the German American Bund operated in the shadow of a foreign government, its claim would be beyond reproach. But the Committee took to defining and categorizing patriotism, thus requiring conformity of a nation founded on divergence of interests and based on freedom. The pursuit of un-Americanism, a convenient catch-all designed to cover any and all prejudices and bias, is inherently un-American itself.

For its part, the Committee credited itself with educating and awakening the American people "to a far better understanding of the sinister character and wide extent of subversive activities."[20] It "justly claim(ed) to have been the decisive force in shaping the . . . attitudes of the American people toward the activities of the 'fifth columns' which aim at our destruction."[21]

Riding the crest of a second world war, America found she could not ignore the cacophony of the radical fringe. Citizens in look-alike uniforms of foreign states elicited tangible fear exhibited in newspaper and radio editorials, pro-American propaganda, and overall mobilization against the perceived threat. For example, in April 1939, Warner Brothers presented "Confessions of a Nazi Spy"—a film which recreated the story of a German spy ring broken in New York City by the FBI in February 1938.[22] Characterizing the German American Bund, in its first week at New York's Strand Theater the film grossed $45,000—more than any previous show that year.[23] The National Board of Review of Motion Pictures named it one of the four best films of the year. America had found a crusade around which to rally.

It was a time of European war and domestic apprehension. In June 1940, President Franklin D. Roosevelt signed a bill requiring all aliens to register with the federal government. The Department of Justice maintained a card file on all potentially suspect Germans. Suspicious German Americans were categorically denied the right to possess arms, wireless sets, transmitters, cameras, military paraphernalia, and the like. Over the course of the decade more than 7,000 were interned on suspicion of espionage. Yet, at the same time, many American school children were saluting the flag with the same outstretched arm as dictated by Nazi ritual.[24]

Was this fear warranted? The German American Bund was a small, isolated, yet vocal sociopolitical group. Its greatest attraction was not of a revolutionary nature—at no time did it advocate the forcible overthrow of the American government. It was a body of culturally-like people—generally recent German immigrants longing for the safety and comfort found in ethnic tradition. That it espoused the doctrine rampant in its mother country is natural. That is not to deny its stance, however. It did heartily echo National Socialism. And, in so doing, presented itself as a representative of Hitler's government.

However, the German American Bund was created

and sustained by Fritz Julius Kuhn—not the German government. Despite Kuhn's braggadocio and Martin Dies' convictions, confirmed administrative or financial links are not to be found between the Party structure in the Third Reich and the Bund. Except for propaganda dispersal, the German American Bund functioned as a true sister movement of the NSDAP. It was a wholly separate entity claiming ties to the same parentage—the doctrine of National Socialism.

Historians are discovering that the Third Reich was not the efficient and highly organized administration, that it seemed to be. Kuhn bragged of his influence over German consular officials and claimed ties to Hitler where in fact neither claim was true. It is likely that the Bund maintained weak and sporadic ties with various personalities or agencies in the Reich without the knowledge of the command group. Benign neglect implies neither avowal nor disavowal. As to the threat of a German fifth column, given the vacillation of American foreign policy and the country's tendency to moral isolationism, it is doubtful that Hitler, or his executive staff, considered the United States as capable of attaining the position of feeding the Third Reich with converts to National Socialism. That they would entertain such an unrealistic belief and assign it to the Bund, given the evidence presented herein, demonstrates the characteristic weakness of the Dies Committee.

The German American Bund was tried and convicted on the basis of the perception it engendered. Its existence broke no laws, nor did it advocate revolutionary principles or the forcible overthrow of the government. What it did advocate was its chosen doctrine—that of National Socialism. Under the First Amendment, its activities were legal and protected by the Constitution.[25] During periods of war or national stress, however, the United States is not adverse to suspending selected freedoms of those it finds potentially threatening. On the one hand, it is a sad, and perhaps unwarranted, aspect of American government. On the other hand, the reaction to the German American Bund, and groups similarly perceived, indicates popular support for the government and for ideal American values. Curiously, America, born of revolution, provides for and allows no avenues for revolt.

The Bund today survives in the minds and hearts of those who lived it. They have carefully preserved the pleasant memories of close camaraderie and cultural comfort that the organization provided them nearly fifty years ago. Most have retreated into social silence, assuming a restricted lifestyle under the limitations of the green card. Many have turned their political allegiance to the current National Socialist White People's Party which is tolerant of and honored by the presence of the august old guard. However, none are active—politically or otherwise. Most are disheartened by the system that cast them aside as unworthy citizens. They feel they have been unjustly maligned—a feeling not uncommon to other minority ethnic groups that were subjected to the intolerance of the decade of the 1930s.

Japanese Americans who underwent the same treatment are beginning to see a change in American opinion. Their mistreatment and total internment was a grave injustice, and finally America attempts to compensate the victims in some small way. For Bundists, however, there are no pardons. Many still live without citizenship and without the property confiscated by the government. The group as a whole was punished for crimes committed by the few due to the solidarity which the group portrayed. The perception of the threat has not died; the image of the Third Reich lives on. And the German American Bund, seen then and now as the New Germany in microcosm, was called upon to pay for the sins of its alleged master.

As for its master in fact, after serving three and a half unglamorous years in prison, Fritz Kuhn was paroled in July 1943. He was immediately dispatched to an internment camp in Crystal City, Texas, to await deportation. There he was joined by his wife Elsa and one of their two children, sixteen year old Walter Kuhn.[26] Kuhn spent a little over two years in various camps of internment. In February 1944, he was transferred from Crystal City to Camp Kenedy, also in Texas. His family had been deported to Germany, and he was moved to a camp for unaccompanied males. He remained there only six months before being transferred to Fort Stanton, New Mexico for disciplinary reasons—officials termed him arrogant, insidious, devious, and politically active.[27]

In September 1945, Kuhn was deported. He sailed for Germany on the SS *Winchester Victory*. It was no victory. Upon his return to his defeated homeland, he was immediately apprehended by United States' authorities and jailed as a war criminal. Released shortly thereafter, he spent a year working in a chemical plant in Munich. In February 1947, he was apprehended by Bavarian authorities and jailed pending a denazification trial.[28] He was released three days later, cleared of all charges.[29] But it was not over. Kuhn was picked up a second time in July, tried for war crimes, and interned in Dachau.[30] He escaped from prison in January 1948 and fled into the French sector where he was picked up six months later.[31] Kuhn appealed the verdict of the courts and was set free in 1950. In 1951, on the ten-year anniversary of the demise of his creation, the German American Bund, Fritz Kuhn died in obscurity. The short and violent journey of the phoenix had ended— the cycle was complete with a return to ashes.

ENDNOTES
Chapter 7

1. This cycle tends to perpetuate itself. See Stanley Coben, "A Study in Nativism: The American Red Scare of 1910-20," *Political Science Quarterly* LXXIX (March 1964): 52-75; John Dewey, "The American Intellectual Frontier," *New Republic*, 10 May 1922: 303-5; John Higham, *Strangers in the Land: Patterns of American Nativism, 1860-1925* (New York: Atheneum, 1963); Don S. Kirschner, *City and Country: Rural Responses to Urbanization in the 1920s* (Westport, Conn.: Greenwood Press, 1970).

2. U. S. Congress, House, 76th Congress, 1st Session, Report #2, Special Committee to Investigate Un-American Activities and Propaganda in the United States, *Investigation of Un-American Activities and Propaganda* (Washington, D. C.: 1939), p. 105. The section on the German American Bund spans pages 91-111.

3. Ibid., p. 105. Kuhn's boast is in reference to the replacement of Ambassador Hans Luther in 1937 by Hans Dieckhoff.

4. Ibid., p. 106.

5. Ibid., pp. 111-114.

6. U. S. Congress, House, 76th Congress, 3rd Session, Report #1476, Special Committee to Investigate Un-American Activities and Propaganda in the United States, *Investigation of Un-American Propaganda Activities in the United States* (Washington, D. C.: 1940), pp. 15-25.

7. Ibid., p. 15. Karl Henlein was the leader of the Nazi group in Czechoslovakia prior to annexation.

8. Ibid., pp. 17-23.

9. Ibid., p. 17.

10. Ibid., p. 21.

11. *New York Times*, 1 September 1939.

12. U. S. Congress, House, 76th Congress, 3rd Session, Report #1476, Special Committee to Investigate Un-American Activities and Propaganda in the United States, *Investigation of Un-American Propaganda Activities in the United States* (Washington, D. C.: 1940), p. 23.

13. U. S. Congress, House, 77th Congress, 1st Session, Special Committee to Investigate Un-American Activities and Propaganda in the United States, *Hearings*, Vol. 14 (Washington, D. C.: 1940), pp. 8251-83 for Kunze's testimony, pp. 8285-8307 for Klapprott's, pp. 8331-8388 for Werner's.

14. U. S. Congress, House, 77th Congress, 1st Session, Report #1, Special Committee to Investigate Un-American Activities and Propaganda in the United States, *Investigation of Un-American Propaganda Activities* (Washington, D. C.: 1941).

15. Ibid., p. 21.

16. Appendix, Part IV of U. S. Congress, House, 77th Congress, 1st Session, Special Committee to Investigate Un-American Activities and Propaganda in the United States, *Special Committee Hearings on Un-American Activities* (Washington, D. C.: 1941), pp. 1490-1620. See also *New York Times*, 2 January 1941.

17. *Washington Post*, 11 January 1940. Also "Dies Committee and True Americanism," *Frontiers of Democracy* 6(1940): 102-4.

18. See Lorraine M. Lees, "National Security and Ethnicity: Contrasting Views During World War II," *Diplomatic History* 11/2 (Spring 1987): 113-125.

19. Concerning Bundists as spies, neither the AO nor the *Abwehr* recruited agents from the German American Bund for fear of damaging relations with the United States. See David Kahn, *Hitler's Spies* (New York: The Macmillan Company, 1978), p. 100. Individual Nazis did spy, however,

most notably G. Wilhelm Kunze. See Ladislas Farago, *The Game of the Foxes: The Untold Story of German Espionage in the United States and Great Britain During World War II* (New York: David McKay Company, Inc., 1971), pp. 319, 428, 435, 442, 454, 502.

20. U. S. Congress, House, 77th Congress, 1st Session, Report #1, Special Committee to Investigate Un-American Activities and Propaganda in the United States, *Investigation of Un-American Propaganda Activities* (Washington, D. C.: 1941), p. 21.

21. Ibid.

22. Eric J. Sandeen, "Confessions of a Nazi Spy and the German American Bund," *American Studies* 20/2 (Fall 1979): 69-81. It is noteworthy to add here that the German government filed protests and banned the film from the Reich. Kuhn filed a $5 million libel suit, in protest of the film, which was later dropped when he was imprisoned.

23. Ibid., p. 73.

24. Taken from "Vignettes of Military History," No. 271, put out by the U. S. Army Military History Institute. The author wishes to thank LTC Alfred J. Davis, USA, who donated the flier to her.

25. The American Civil Liberties Union was an active supporter of the Bund's (and earlier the Friends') civil rights. Although the ACLU was not, in any way, sympathetic to the Bund's views, it crusaded stridently for their protection and freedoms. For a chronicle of ACLU-Bund activity, see Martha Glaser, "The German American Bund in New Jersey," *New Jersey History* 92/1 (1974): 33-49.

26. Taken from Kuhn's "Enemy Alien Questionnaire" which he was required to fill out upon internment. Courtesy U. S. Department of Justice.

27. Ibid.

28. *New York Times*, 2 February 1947.

29. *New York Times*, 5 February 1947.

30. Ibid., 18, 25 July 1947.

31. "Fritz Kuhn verhaftet," *Tagesspiegel* (Germany), 18 June 1948.

SELECTED
BIBLIOGRAPHY

Primary Sources

Dennis, Lawrence. *The Coming of American Fascism.* New York: AMS Press, 1977.

Deutscher Weckruf und Beobachter. 1936-1938.

Dies, Martin. *The Trojan Horse in America.* New York: Dodd, Mead and Co., 1940.

Dodd, Martha and William E. *Ambassador Dodd's Diary 1933-38.* New York: Harcourt, Brace and Company, 1941.

Minutes of the 1938 National Convention of the German American Bund.

New York Evening Journal. 1934-1938.

New York Times. 1934-1941.

Smith, Alson J. "I Went to a Nazi Rally." *Christian Century* 56 (8 March 1939): 320-322.

Suitland, Maryland. National Archives. Record Group 131. Records of the German American Bund.

U. S. Congress. House. *Hearings.* Vol. I, 75th Congress, 3rd session, 1938.

_____. *Investigation of Nazi and Other Propaganda.* 74th Congress, 1st session, 1935.

_____. *Investigation of Un-American Activities and Propaganda.* 76th Congress, 1st session, 1939.

_____. *Investigation of Un-American Propaganda Activities in the United States.* House report 2, 76th Congress, 1st session, 1939.

_____. *Investigation of Un-American Propaganda Activities in the United States.* House report 1476, 76th Congress, 3rd session, 1940.

_____. *Investigation of Un-American Propaganda Activities.* House report 1, 77th Congress, 1st session, 1941.

_____. *Special Committee Hearings on Un-American Activities.* Appendix, part IV, 77th Congress, 1st session, 1941.

U. S. Department of Justice. "Outline of Evidence." *The German American Bund.* September 17, 1942.

U. S. Department of State. *Documents on German Foreign Policies, 1918-1945, from the Archives of the German Foreign Ministry.* Series C,D. Washington, D. C.: 1949-50.

_____. *Foreign Relations of the United States, 1938.* Washington, D. C.: 1955.

Secondary Sources

Allen, Frederick Lewis. *Only Yesterday: An Informal History of the 1920s.* Norwood, Pa.: Telegraph Books, 1931.

Archer, Jules. *The Plot to Seize the White House.* New York: Hawthorn Books, Inc., 1973.

Bell, Daniel. *Marxian Socialism in the United States.* Princeton: Princeton University Press, 1967.

Bell, Leland V. *In Hitler's Shadow: The Anatomy of American Nazism.* New York: Kennikat Press, 1973.

Bennett, David. *Demogogues in the Depression.* New Brunswick, N. J.: Rutgers University Press, 1969.

Bracher, Karl Dietrich. *The German Dictatorship: The Origins, Structure, and Effects of National Socialism.* New York: Holt, Rinehart and Winston, 1970.

Brinkley, Alan. *Voices of Protest.* New York: Vintage Books, 1982.

Carlson, John. *Under Cover.* New York: E. P. Dutton and Co., Inc., 1943.

Carr, Robert K. *The House Committee on Un-American Activities.* New York: Cornell University Press, 1952.

Chafee, Zechariah, Jr. *Free Speech in the United States.* Cambridge: Harvard University Press, 1941.

Child, Clifton J. *The German-Americans in Politics.* New York: Arno Press and the New York Times, 1970.

Compton, James V. *The Swastika and the Eagle: Hitler, the United States, and the Origins of World War II.* Boston: Houghton Mifflin Co., 1967.

Craig, Cordon A. *The Germans.* New York: G. P. Putnam's Sons, 1982.

Craig, Gordon A., and Holborn, Hajo, eds. *The Diplomats 1919-1939.* New Jersey: Princeton University Press, 1953.

DeJong, Louis. *The German Fifth Column in the Second World War.* Chicago: University of Chicago Press, 1956.

Devlin, Patrick. *Too Proud to Fight: Woodrow Wilson's Neutrality.* New York: Oxford University Press, 1975.

DeWeerd, Harvey A. *President Wilson Fights His War: World War I and the American Intervention.* New York: The Macmillan Company, 1968.

Diamond, Sander A. *The Nazi Movement in the United States 1924-1941*. Ithaca: Cornell University Press, 1974.

Faust, Albert B. *The German Element in the United States*. Salem, N. H.: Ayer Company Publishers, Inc., 1927.

Friedlander, Saul. *Prelude to Downfall: Hitler and the United States 1939-1941*. London: Chatto and Windus, 1967.

Friedrich, Otto. *Before the Deluge*. New York: Avon, 1973.

Frye, Alton. *Nazi Germany and the American Hemisphere*. New Haven: Yale University Press, 1967.

Galbraith, John Kenneth. *The Great Crash: 1929*. New York: Time Incorporated, 1954.

Gerson, Louis L. *The Hyphenate in Recent American Politics and Diplomacy*. Lawrence: University of Kansas Press, 1964.

Glaser, Martha. "The German American Bund in New Jersey." *New Jersey History* 92/1 (1974): 33-49.

Goodman, Walter. *The Committee*. New York: Farrar, Straus and Giroux, 1968.

Gregory, Ross. *The Origins of American Intervention in the First World War*. New York: W. W. Norton and Company, Inc., 1971.

Hartmann, Edward George. *The Movement to Americanize the Immigrant*. New York: AMS Press, 1967.

Higham, John. *Send These to Me: Jews and Other Immigrants in Urban America*. New York: Atheneum, 1975.

———. *Strangers in the Land: Patterns of American Nativism, 1860-1925*. New York: Atheneum, 1963.

Huebener, Theodore. *The Germans in America*. New York: Chilton Co., 1962.

Johnson, Niel M. *George Sylvester Viereck*. Chicago: University of Illinois Press, 1972.

Johnson, Ronald W. "German American Bund and Nazi Germany, 1936-1941." *Studies in History and Society* 6/2 (1975): 31-45.

Jones, Kenneth Paul, ed. *U. S. Diplomats in Europe 1919-1941*. Oxford: Clio Press, 1981.

Kennedy, David M. *Over Here: The First World War and American Society*. New York: Oxford University Press, 1980.

Kimball, Warren F. "Dieckhoff and America: A German's View of German-American Relations, 1937-1941." *The Historian* 27/2 (1965): 218-243.

Kirschner, Don S. *City and Country: Rural Responses to Urbanization in the 1920s*. Westport, Conn.: Greenwood Press, 1970.

Klehr, Harvey K. *The Heyday of American Communism: The Depression Decade*. New York: Basic Books, 1935.

Lasswell, Harold D. *Propaganda Technique in World War I*. Cambridge: The M.I.T. Press, 1971.

Ledeboer, Suzanne C. "The Man Who Would Be Hitler: William Dudley Pelley." *California History* 65 (June 1986): 126-136.

Leuchtenburg, William E. *Franklin Delano Roosevelt and the New Deal, 1932-1940.* New York: Harper and Row, 1963.

_____. *The Perils of Prosperity, 1914-1933.* Chicago: University of Chicago Press, 1948.

Luebke, Frederick C. *Bonds of Loyalty: German-Americans and World War I.* DeKalb: Northern Illinois Press, 1974.

McKale, Donald M. *The Swastika Outside Germany.* Ohio: Kent State University Press, 1977.

Mock, James R., and Larson, Cedric. *Words that Won the War: The Story of the Committee on Public Information, 1917-1919.* Princeton: Princeton University Press, 1939.

Murphy, Paul L. *World War I and the Origin of Civil Liberties in the U. S.* New York: W. W. Norton and Company, 1979.

Noggle, Burl. *Into the Twenties: The United States from Armistice to Normalcy.* Chicago: University of Illinois Press, 1974.

O'Connor, Richard. *The German Americans.* Boston: Little, Brown and Company, 1968.

Offner, Arnold A. *The Origins of the Second World War: American Foreign Policy and World Politics, 1917-1941.* New York: Praeger Publishers, 1975.

Ogden, August Raymond. *The Dies Committee: A Study of the Special House Committee for the Investigation of Un-American Activities, 1938-1944.* Washington, D. C.: The Catholic University of America Press, 1945.

Parmet, Robert D. *Labor and Immigration in Industrial America*. Boston: Twayne Publishers, 1981.

Pells, Richard. *Radical Visions and American Dreams: Culture and Social Thought in the Depression Years*. Middletown, Conn.: Wesleyan University Press, 1977.

Perrett, Geoffrey. *America in the Twenties*. New York: Simon and Schuster, 1982.

Peterson, H. C. *Opponents of War 1917-1918: The Story of the Persecution of Anti-War Groups*. Seattle: University of Washington Press, 1968.

————. *Propaganda for War: The Campaign against American Neutrality, 1914-1917*. Norman: University of Oklahoma Press, 1939.

Preston, William Jr. *Aliens and Dissenters: Federal Suppression of Radicals, 1903-1933*. New York: Harper and Row, 1966.

Remak, Joachim. "Friends of the New Germany: The Bund and German-American Relations." *Journal of Modern History* 29 (March 1957): 38-41.

Rippley, LaVern J. *The German Americans*. Boston: Twayne Publishers, 1976.

Roberts, Stephen H. *The House that Hitler Built*. New York: Harper and Brothers, Publishers, 1938.

Rogge, O. John. *The Official German Report*. New York: Thomas Yoseloff, 1961.

Romasco, Albert U. *The Poverty of Abundance: Hoover, the Nation, and the Depression*. New York: Oxford University Press, 1965.

Sandeen, Eric J. "Confessions of a Nazi Spy and the German American Bund." *American Studies* 20/2 (Fall 1979): 69-81.

Sanders, M. L., and Taylor, Philip M. *British Propaganda during the First World War, 1914-18.* Stanford: Stanford University Press, 1938.

Schalk, Adolph. *The Germans.* New Jersey: Prentice-Hall, Inc., 1971.

Scheiber, Harry N. *The Wilson Administration and Civil Liberties, 1917-1921.* Ithaca: Cornell University Press, 1960.

Schlesinger, Arthur M., Jr. *The Coming of the New Deal.* Boston: Houghton Mifflin Company, 1959.

_____. *The Crisis of the Old Order, 1919-1933.* Boston: Houghton Mifflin Company, 1957.

Seller, Maxine. *To Seek America: A History of Ethnic Life in the United States.* Englewood, N. J.: Jerome S. Ozer, 1977.

Shannon, David A. *The Socialist Party of America.* New York: Quadrangle Books, Inc., 1955.

Smith, Geoffrey S. *To Save a Nation: American Countersubversives, the New Deal, and the Coming of World War II.* New York: Basic Books, 1972.

Sobel, Robert. *The Great Bull Market: Wall Street in the 1920s.* New York: W. W. Norton and Company, Inc., 1968.

Sowell, Thomas. *Ethnic America.* New York: Basic Books, Inc., 1981.

Stone, Albert, Jr. "Seward Collins and the *American Review*: Experiment in Pro-Fascism 1933-1937." *American Quarterly* XII (1960): 3-19.

Swing, Raymond Gram. *Forerunners of American Fascism*. New York: Books for Libraries Press, 1935.

Warren, Frank A. *An Alternative Vision: The Socialist Party in the 1930s*. Bloomington: Indiana University Press, 1974.

Weinberg, Gerhard L. *The Foreign Policy of Hitler's Germany, 1933-1936*. Chicago: University of Chicago Press, 1971.

Wittke, Carl. *We Who Built America: The Saga of the Immigrant*. Cleveland: Press of Case Western Reserve University, 1964.

Woolston, Howard B. "Rating the Nations: A Study in the Statistics of Opinion." *American Journal of Sociology* 22 (November 1916): 381-90.

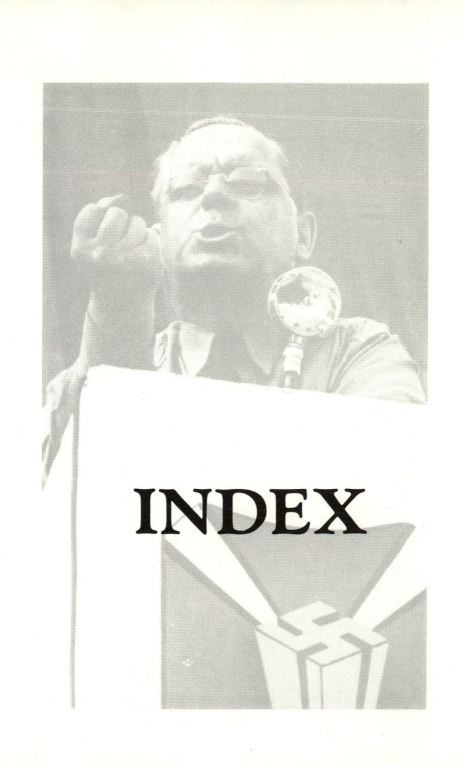

INDEX

INDEX

GLOSSARY

GLOSSARY

AO, Auslands Organisation
    Organization for Foreigners

APA, Aussenpolitisches Amt
    Foreign Policy Office

AV, Amerikadeutscher Volksbund
    German-American People's Organization

Bund
    League, union or alliance bound by covenant

DAI, Deutsches Auslands Institut
    German Foreign Institute

DAWA, Deutsch-Amerikanischer Wirtschafts Ausschuss
    German-American Protective Alliance

DKV, Deutscher Konsum Verband
    German Business League

Fuehrerprinzip
    Ideology of dominant authoritarian leadership

Gau
    Political administrative district

HUAC
    House Un-American Activities Committee

250

*NSDAP, Nationalsozialistische Deutsche
Arbeiterpartei*
Nazis—National Socialist German Workers Party

OD, Ordnungsdienst
Security Force

VDA, Verein fuer das Deutschtum im Ausland
League of Germans Abroad

All photographs are from the collection of the National Archives, Washington DC

- design and graphic production by John R. Kirschner
- cover design by Michael Craft
- typeset in Century Schoolbook by Comp-Type, Inc., Fort Bragg, California
- printed on recycled neutral pH papers by The Robots, Inc., Mtn View, California
- binding by Special Editions, Stockton, California